CONVERSE® ALL STAR™
BASEBALL
HOW TO PLAY LIKE A PRO

DATE DUE

A MOUNTAIN LION BOOK

John Wiley & Sons, Inc.
New York • Chichester • Weinheim • Brisbane • Singapore • Toronto

Copyright © 1997 by Mountain Lion, Inc.
Published by John Wiley & Sons, Inc.

In order to keep the instructions in this book as simple as possible, the word "he" is used to mean either boys or girls.

The publisher and the author have made every reasonable effort to insure that the activities in the book are safe when conducted as instructed but assume no responsibility for any damage caused or sustained while performing the activities in this book. Parents, guardians, and/or coaches should supervise young readers who undertake the activities in this book.

Library of Congress Cataloging-in-Publication Data

Converse all star baseball : how to play like a pro.
     p. cm. — (The Converse all star sports series)
  "A Mountain Lion book."
  Summary: Provides instructions for young players on all aspects of baseball, including batting, running the bases, pitching, catching, and fielding.
  Includes bibliographical references (p.).
  ISBN 0-471-15991-3 (pbk. : alk. paper)
  1. Baseball—Training—Juvenile literature. [1. Baseball.]
I. Converse (Firm) II. Series.
GV875.6.C66 1997
796.357'07—dc20   96-46583

Printed in the United States of America
10 9 8 7 6 5 4 3 2 1

CONTENTS

Games using a ball have been around almost as long as man himself. Ancient Egyptian paintings show two people rolling a ball back and forth. The Egyptians, Greeks, and Romans played games in which a ball was hit with a stick. In Europe, ball-and-stick games have been played for centuries.

The first settlers that came to America brought their games with them. Ball-and-stick games were played differently in different parts of the country, but they had one thing in common: They were played by hitting a pitched ball with a stick or bat, then running around a series of bases to get "home." Towns played against other towns. Amateur baseball clubs were formed.

In 1845, the New York Knickerbocker Baseball Club adopted a set of rules that were written down by Alexander Cartwright. The rules described the playing field and called for an umpire to settle disputes. The ball was always thrown under-handed, and a game lasted until one team scored 21 points.

The first professional baseball team, the Cincinnati Red Stockings, was formed in 1869. They toured the country playing against local teams. America was in love with baseball. In 1876, the National League was organized. The rules of baseball continued to change, as the game's players made baseball into America's own sport. The first overhand pitch was thrown in 1884. By 1900, the game was pretty much the way we know it today.

America is still in love with baseball. There are professional leagues and amateur leagues. There are college, high school, and youth baseball teams. Still, some of the best games are played with friends in fields and empty lots.

The chapters in this book tell you how to learn all the skills you need to become a good player. You'll find help with pitching, batting, and fielding. You'll find drills and games that make practicing fun. Use this book to learn to play like a pro. Then teach your friends!

CHAPTER 1

This Game Called Baseball

Baseball is a game for everyone. You don't have to be 200 pounds of solid muscle. You don't have to be six feet tall. Most baseball players have average bodies that they've gotten into shape by training and practice. To play baseball, a boy or girl needs good coordination (ability to move quickly and easily). The rest of the skills you need can be learned by reading this book, playing the game, and practicing—a lot.

Getting Started

The best place to start is to learn a little about the game and how it's played.

The Aim of the Game

In a baseball game, two teams of nine players each try to score by hitting the ball with a bat, then running around a series of four bases while the other team tries to stop them by putting them out of the game.

Baseball Is a Team Sport

One reason why baseball is so popular is that it's a team sport. Each team member has a job to do, but he must also work with his teammates. The best baseball teams are made up of good players who know how to play together to be great. Together, teammates can do something they can't do alone—win.

Ball, Bat, and Glove

The baseball has a center made out of cork that is wrapped with layers of wool and cotton yarns, which are covered with two pieces of cowhide that are sewn together. The ball is 9 to 9½ inches around and weighs between 5 and 5¼ ounces.

Bats are made of wood or aluminum. They are not permitted to be more than 42 inches in length, or greater than 2¾ inches in circumference. For young players, bats are usually no longer than 34 inches and not heavier than 30 ounces. The days when Babe Ruth used to swing a 38-inch, 42-ounce piece of lumber have long since passed.

Gloves and mitts are usually made of leather pieces stitched together along the outer edges to form a pocket over the palm. The pocket holds the ball in place once it has been caught. Gloves have separations for the fingers. Mitts have no separations for the fingers. Catchers and first basemen wear mitts, and the other players wear gloves. (The positions of catcher and first baseman are explained later in this chapter.)

The Field

The playing *field* is made up of an infield, an outfield, and foul territories (Figure 1).

The Infield

The *infield*, also called the *diamond*, is a square area with a *base* in each corner. Bases are first, second, third, and home plate. First, second, and third bases are made of stuffed, rectangular pads that are fastened to the ground. *Home plate* is a white, five-sided, rubber plate that is level with the ground. On a professional baseball field, the bases are 90 feet apart. The distances are shorter for young players.

Directly behind home plate is an area called the *catcher's box*, and near the dugouts are the *on-deck circles*.

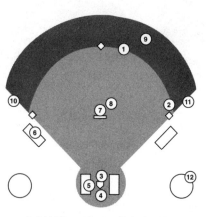

1. Infield (diamond)	7. Pitcher's rubber
2. Base	8. Pitcher's mound
3. Home plate	9. Outfield
4. Catcher's box	10. Foul line
5. Batter's box	11. Foul territory
6. Coaches' box	12. On-deck circles

There are several areas on the baseball field that a young ballplayer should be familiar with before he plays the game.

On each side of home plate is a four-foot-by-six-foot rectangle, called a *batter's box*. The batter's box to the left of the plate is for right-handed batters. The batter's box to the right of the plate is for left-handed batters.

On the outside of the diamond, near first base, and near third base, are two rectangular areas called *coaching boxes*.

Sixty feet and six inches from home plate is the *pitcher's rubber*, which is located on the *pitcher's mound*.

1-1: Camden Yards is the home field of the Baltimore Orioles. It's regarded as one of the finest stadiums in major league baseball.

The Outfield

The *outfield* is the wide area surrounding the diamond from first to second base and from second to third base. In professional ballparks, there's a fence at the edge of the outfield. The shape and size of the outfield can vary. In a professional ballpark, the outfield fence should be at least 325 feet from home plate.

Foul and Fair Territories

Two foul lines start at home plate and run past first and third bases to the far edges of the outfield. The area inside the foul lines is called fair territory. Any area outside the foul lines is called foul territory.

Offense and Defense

When your team is playing *offense*, they are *at bat*, meaning your team's players are taking turns *batting* (hitting the ball with the bat). When your team is playing *defense*, then the other team is at bat and your team is *in the field*, trying to stop them from scoring.

1-2: A hitter should stretch and take some practice swings while he's in the on-deck circle. It's also a great place to monitor the pitcher.

Innings

When each team has had a turn at bat and a turn in the field, an *inning* has been completed. A professional baseball game lasts for nine innings. In youth baseball, fewer than nine innings are played.

Scoring

A run is scored when a player touches first, second, third, and home plate in turn (Figure 1-3). The team with the most runs at the end of the game wins. The game never ends in a tie. If there is a tie score at the end of the last inning, extra innings are played until the tie is broken.

1-3: It takes a team effort to score runs in baseball. Boston Red Sox slugger Mo Vaughn congratulates teammate John Valentin after crossing the plate.

The Players

When your team is playing in the field, each player has a special job to do. The defensive playing positions are:

The Battery

The battery is the name given to the pitcher and catcher together.

- **Pitcher.** The player who stands on the pitcher's mound and pitches (throws) the ball to the batter.
- **Catcher.** The player who crouches behind home plate and receives the ball from the pitcher when it is not hit by the batter.

Infield

Infielders are the four players who cover the infield.

- **First Baseman.** The player who covers first base and the area around it.
- **Second Baseman.** The player who covers second base and the area from second base toward first base.
- **Shortstop.** The player who covers the area between second and third base. He also covers second base as a partner to the second baseman.
- **Third Baseman.** The player who covers third base and the area around it.

Outfield

Outfielders are the three players who play in the outfield.

- **Right Fielder.** The player who covers the area beyond first base from the right foul line to the area covered by the center fielder.
- **Left Fielder.** The player who covers the area beyond third base from the left foul line to the area covered by the center fielder.
- **Center Fielder.** The player who covers the area in the middle of the outfield beyond second base.

Playing the Game

Before the game begins, the manager of each team decides on a *batting order*, which is the order in which the players will bat. The batting order is written down and given to the umpire before the game begins. The batting order may not be changed during the game.

The *home team* (whose field the game is played on) takes their defensive positions on the field. The first batter for the visiting team comes to the batter's box, the umpire calls out "play ball," and the pitcher pitches the first ball to the catcher.

If the ball is thrown inside the *strike zone* (the area above home plate that is between the batter's armpits and knee tops) and the batter doesn't swing at the ball, or if he swings at any pitch and misses, it's called a *strike* (Figure 1-4). After the batter takes three strikes, he's *out*, meaning his turn at bat is over (also called *striking out*).

When the ball is hit by the batter, it can be either a foul ball or a fair ball. A *foul ball* is one that goes into foul territory. A foul ball is also a strike, except when the batter already has two strikes. (You can't strike out on a foul ball.)

A *fair ball* is one that is goes into fair territory. On fair balls, the batter, and any other players who are already on a base, may advance around the bases as far as they can while the ball is in play. A runner is *safe* when he reaches a base and stops there before the play ends.

When a team has three outs, their turn at bat ends and they move to play defense in the field while the other team is at bat.

Outside the Lines

THE HISTORY OF STRIKES AND BALLS
In 1876, batters were allowed three strikes and nine balls. The next season the rule was changed to four strikes, but finally, in 1889, the rule was set at four balls and three strikes.

Rules and Terms

Ball

If the ball is thrown outside the strike zone and the batter doesn't swing, it's called a *ball*. After four balls, the batter gets to walk to first base, called a *walk* or a *base on balls*.

Hit

A fair ball that allows the runner to reach a base safely is called a *hit*. A hit that allows the batter to advance one base is called a *single*. A two-base hit is called a *double*, a three-base hit is called a *triple*, and a four-base hit is called a *home run*.

Fly Ball

A *fly ball* is a batted ball that travels high in the air. A *pop fly* only travels as far as the infield.

1-4: The umpire judges each pitch and calls the balls and strikes.

Forced to Run

When there's a runner on first, or runners on first and second, or runners on first, second, and third, and a fair ball hits the ground, each runner must advance to the next base because two runners can't be on the same base at the same time.

Putouts

You already know that when a batter gets three strikes, he's out. A *putout* is when an offensive player is put out of the game because of a play by the defense. Here's three kinds of putouts:

1. The batter is out when a defensive player catches a fair or foul ball before it touches the ground.

2. The runner is out when a defensive player tags the runner with the ball or with the glove that has the ball in it before he reaches base.

3. The runner is out when a fielder tags the base in front of the runner when he's been forced to run.

Double Play

A double play is when the defense puts out two offensive players on one hit ball.

Sacrifice

When the batter hits the ball to get one of his team's runners to the next base, even though the batter, himself, gets put out, it's called a *sacrifice* (Figure 1-5).

Error

When a member of the defensive team makes a fielding or throwing mistake that allows a runner to advance a base or to score, it's called an *error*.

1-5: Philadelphia Phillies Mickey Morandini is shown here laying down a sacrifice bunt.

Obstructing the Runner

If any member of the fielding team obstructs (gets in the way of) a runner's path, the runner gets to advance to one base beyond the last one he legally touched.

Balk Rule

Once the pitcher has his foot (or toes) on the pitcher's plate and has started his *windup* (bringing his throwing arm back before pitching), he must continue his motion and pitch the ball to the plate. If one or more runners are on base and the pitcher fails to finish the pitch, it's called a balk. A pitcher can balk by stopping his pitch, dropping the ball, or throwing to a base. When the pitcher balks, each runner advances one base.

The Officials

During a game, an official scorer keeps track of hits, runs, and errors. Umpires enforce the rules of the game and call balls and strikes. In professional baseball, there are four umpires, one at home plate and one near each base.

Manager and Coaches

The manager is in charge of the team during a game (Figure 1-6). He makes decisions on the batting order and *strategy* (the game plan). A coach is the manager's assistant. There can be more than one coach for a team. Coaches teach hitting, pitching, and fielding.

Pro Baseball

Professional, or *pro*, baseball players earn their living by playing baseball. In the United States, pros play in the major leagues and minor leagues.

Major and Minor Leagues
The *major leagues* are made up the *American League* and the *National League*, each of which has 14 professional teams. The *minor* leagues are made up of teams that are used for training promising professional players who may later advance to major league teams. Some minor league teams are associated with certain major league teams. These minor league teams are called *farm teams*.

1-6: Tony LaRussa is one of the brightest managers in the major leagues. In his first season in St. Louis, LaRussa led the Cardinals to the National League Central Division title.

League Champions and the World Series
At the end of each baseball season, playoffs are held to determine the American League and National League champions. Then the two league champions play each other in the *World Series*. The first team to win four games is the winner and is the world champion team for that year.

Baseball players have to move fast, be strong, and have *endurance* (the ability to keep going for a long time). Being in top physical shape also helps protect you from getting hurt when you play. Each training session should start with a warm-up, followed by stretching, followed by strength and endurance exercises (Figures 1-7 and 1-8).

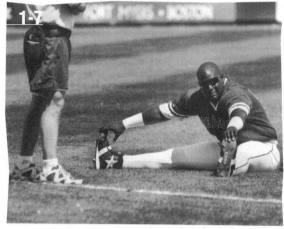

1-7: It's very important to stretch before practice and games. Loosening the muscles and having flexibility makes you a better player and can help you avoid injuries.

Warm-up and Stretch

Stretching your muscles makes you more flexible (able to move easily). Never stretch a cold muscle. Take a short jog to warm up before starting to stretch.

When you stretch, keep your body relaxed and take long, slow breaths. Stretching should feel good. Hold each stretch for at least 10 seconds and don't stretch so far that you feel pain. If stretching is painful, stop and get advice from your coach.

Leg Stretching

1. While standing up, lift one foot off the ground. Hold your leg still and move your foot in a circle while you count to eight, then switch legs.

2. Lift one foot up behind you and grab the ankle. Push your foot out away from your hand until you feel a stretch down the front of your thigh. Count to five, then change legs.

3. Stand with your legs a shoulder's width apart. Touch the toes of one foot with the fingers of the opposite arm. Then use your other hand to touch the toes of the other foot. Keep switching arms until you have done 30 touches.

Middle Body and Arm Stretching

1. **The Side Twister.** Stand up and lay a bat across your shoulders (behind your head). Hold the bat near each end with your hands (your arms should be out beside you with elbows bent). Keep your hips facing forward and twist your upper body to the right, then back to the left, then to the right, and so on. Do ten twists to each side.

2. **Arm Circles.** Stand with your arms straight out to the sides. Make forward circles with your arms while you count to ten. Then count to ten while you make backward circles.

1-8: Always stretch your arms before throwing or hitting. Even all-stars like catcher Mike Piazza can get a sore arm if he doesn't properly stretch.

3. Hold one arm across your chest. Grab the tricep with the other arm and pull it until you feel a stretch (Figure 1-8). Hold for ten seconds and then switch arms.

Strength Training

Young players under the age of 14 shouldn't lift weights or use weight machines. If you want to lift weights when you are old enough, train with someone who knows how to use weights the correct way for a baseball player (Figure 1-9). (Not every weight-lifting program is good for baseball players.)

Here are some exercises that help you build strength:

1. **Push-ups.** Get down on your hands (palms flat on the ground) and toes with your legs straight out behind you. Keep your hands under your shoulders. Keeping your body straight, bend your elbows to lower your chest toward the floor, then push back up. Do 10 push-ups at first. You can increase the number of push-ups as you get stronger.

2. **Sit-ups.** Lie down on your back with your knees bent and your feet flat on the floor. Cross your arms over your chest with your hands on your shoulders. Lift your shoulders off the floor and start to sit up. Come up just far enough to feel your stomach muscles tighten. Ease back a little toward the floor, then pull up again. Repeat 10 times. You can increase the number of sit-ups as you get stronger.

3. **Squeeze Ball.** To build strength in your hands, squeeze a rubber ball in one hand over and over for two minutes, then switch hands.

Endurance Training

One way to build endurance is to go for long runs. Be sure to warm up and stretch before running. On your first run, go as far as you can until you get tired and out of breath. Stop running if you have pain anywhere in your body. Each time, try to run a little farther until you can run five miles without getting tired.

Speed Training

Do some sprinting (running fast for a short distance). You can practice sprinting from base to base on an empty field, or during your long run, you can suddenly speed up for a short distance, then slow back down (Figure 1-10).

1-9: Strength training has certainly helped Jose Canseco's baseball career. Here he shows you exactly what can be gained through hard work in the weight room.

1-10: You've got to be in great shape to play every day. No one knows that better than Cal Ripken, Jr.

Make It Up, Play It Out

Playing catch with a baseball is a good way to get a feel for the ball and glove.

Baseball Catch

You need two players, two gloves, a baseball, and markers such as caps, cones, or flags. Mark off the corners of two three-foot squares, about twelve feet apart. The players, each wearing a glove, stand in the squares and throw the ball back and forth to each other. Players throw overhand (bring your arm back, then move it forward above your shoulder as you throw). The ball must be caught in the glove. If a thrower tosses the ball into the receiver's square and the receiver fails to catch it, then the thrower gets a point. If a thrower tosses the ball outside the receiver's square and the receiver fails to catch it, the receiver gets a point. The player with the most points wins the game.

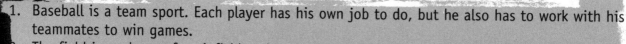

Keep Focused

1. Baseball is a team sport. Each player has his own job to do, but he also has to work with his teammates to win games.
2. The field is made up of an infield and an outfield with fair and foul territories.
3. When your team is playing offense, they are at bat.
4. When your team is playing defense, they are in the field, trying to stop the other team from scoring.
5. A run is scored when a player touches first, second, third, and home plate in turn.
6. A strike occurs when the ball is thrown inside the strike zone and the batter doesn't swing at it, or when the batter swings at any pitch but misses the ball.
7. A hit that allows the runner to advance one base is called a single. A two-base hit is a double, a three-base hit is a triple, and a four-base hit is a home run.
8. A ball occurs when the pitch is thrown outside the strike zone and the batter doesn't take a swing. A player walks on four balls.

2

Batting

Y ou're in the batter's box. The pitcher fires the ball. You've got less than a second to judge your aim. The ball is small. It's coming straight at you. No. It's dropping down. You swing. You hear the crack of the bat. Your arms feel the force of the hit. It feels just right—you know it's a good hit.

Every player takes his place in the batting order. No matter what field position you play, you're a batter for your team. When you step up to the plate to face the pitcher, it's up to you to get on base or to advance your teammates who are already on base.

Ted Williams, one of baseball's greatest hitters, said that hitting a baseball was the hardest thing to do in sports. Maybe that's because there's no one best way to hit a baseball. Great hitters each have their own style (way) of batting. If you want to be a great hitter, you have to find the style that works best for you. To find that style, learn the basics of batting and work with your body to make the most of your own special strengths. Then practice, practice, practice your swing.

Find the Right Bat

The small end of the bat is the *handle* and the fat end is the *barrel*. Bats come in different weights and lengths. To find the one that's just right for you, pick up many bats, one after the other. Find one that's light enough for you to swing fast, yet heavy enough to hit the ball with power. The bat should feel comfortable in your hands (Figure 2-1).

2-1: Try holding the bat out parallel to the ground with one arm. If you can do it without trouble, you've got a bat that you can handle.

Most wooden bats are made from white ash, a strong, hard wood that has some *give*. Give means that the bat is just a little bit flexible, which helps it take the shock of a pitched ball. Professional ball players use only wooden bats. Even though wooden bats are very strong, they sometimes break. A major league hitter can go through as many as 60 bats in a season.

Aluminum bats don't have the give of wooden bats, but they are very popular with young players. Aluminum bats almost never break, and because they are hollow, they can have a bigger barrel and still be light enough to swing fast. Sometimes aluminum bats can sting your fingers when you hit the ball. Wrapping the handle with tape will help take the sting out of a hit.

Get a Grip

Grip (grab) the bat by the handle. Right-handed hitters keep the right hand on top. Left-handed hitters keep the left hand on top. Keep your palms against the bat and line up the second knuckle of your top hand between the second and third knuckles of your bottom hand (Figure 2-2).

Where you place your hands on the bat is part of your style. The more you choke up on the bat (get closer to the barrel), the lighter the bat feels and the shorter the bat becomes (Figure 2-3). Shortening the bat a little gives you more speed. More speed means more power.

To get a better grip on the bat, some players rub their bats with pine tar, which is sticky stuff that comes from a pine tree. Some batters wear special batting gloves to get a better grip.

2-2: The bat should always be gripped loosely and in the fingers. Eliminate any tension in the hands and wrists. The second set of knuckles in the top hand should lie somewhere between the second and third knuckles of the bottom hand.

Take a Stand in the Batter's Box

There are two batter's boxes near home plate. If you're a right-handed batter, stand in the batter's box to the left of the plate. If you're a left-handed batter, stand in the batter's box to the right of the plate.

Place yourself in the batter's box so it's easy to swing the bat over home plate. Make sure that you have enough room in front of you to take a *stride* (step) forward when you swing. If your foot goes outside the batter's box while you swing, you're out.

Your Feet

There are three basic types of *stances* (ways of standing in the box):

The Square Stance

The *square stance* (Figure 2-4) means that your feet are at a right angle to the pitcher and about a shoulder's width apart. The square stance is popular with young players. It allows you to reach most kinds of pitches.

2-3: A hitter doesn't sacrifice power when he chokes up on the bat. Barry Bonds chokes up on his bat with every swing, and he certainly packs plenty of power.

2-4: The hitter is using a square stance in this photo. This is the best stance for a hitter who is just getting started. 2-5: The open stance is often used when the hitter has trouble handling the inside strike. Although the front foot is opened, the stride should still go directly back at the pitcher. 2-6: The closed stance gives the hitter good plate coverage on pitches from the middle to the outside part of the plate. Make sure you turn your head and use both eyes.

The Closed Stance

In the *closed stance* (Figure 2-5) your front foot is closer to the plate than your back foot. This closes your body (turns your shoulder) toward the pitcher.

The Open Stance

In the *open stance* (Figure 2-6) your back foot is closer to the plate than your front foot. This opens your body (turns the front of your body) to the pitcher.

Try all the different stances. Go with the one that works best for you.

Your Body

No matter which stance you use, keep your weight on the balls of your feet. Bend your knees and crouch a little (Figure 2-7). Turn your head so that both eyes are looking at the pitcher. Keep your eyes level and your head still.

Your Arms

Hold your bat about three to six inches away from your body. Keep your hands above your back foot and even with your chest. Some hitters like to hold their bat with the barrel straight up in the air. Other hitters like to hold their bat almost horizontal to the ground. Experiment with different bat positions until you find what works best for you.

2-7, 2-8: Ken Caminiti uses somewhat of an awkward stance. His hands are held low and in towards his body, and his knees are bent in a crouched position. However, once he strides, he's set in the launch position. In the launch position the front foot plants from the stride and the hands are cocked back ready to start the swing.

Find Your Swing

Here's seven steps to a good, basic swing:

1. When the pitcher goes into his windup, *shift your weight to your back foot and cock your hands* (bend your wrists toward your back).

2. Watch the ball leave the pitcher's hand as you pick up your front foot and *stride toward the pitcher, keeping the weight on your back foot* (Figure 2-8). This puts all the power of your back, shoulders, and arms into your swing. The stride starts the rest of your body in motion.

3. When your front foot comes down, *turn your hips toward the pitcher and move your hands forward through the swing*. Keep your shoulders level as you swing. You should still have your eye on the ball (Figure 2-9).

2-9: Before the bat comes through the hitting zone, the hitter should point the knob of the bat at the ball. This puts the bat on line with the ball. 2-10: Keep the head down on the ball right up until the point of contact. Notice this hitter's hands are in the "palm up, palm down" position when contact is made. 2-11: Always try to hit the ball where it's pitched. This hitter takes an outside pitch and drives it to right field. He waits until the ball is back in the hitting zone instead of getting it out front as you would do on the inside pitch. 2-12: Follow all the way through on your swing. If you cut your swing short, you'll sacrfice power.

4. *Hit the ball with the* hitting area *of your bat* (an area on the barrel, about a foot long, that starts about two inches from the top). This area of the bat is called the *sweet spot* (Figure 2-10) because it's where you get the most power. (The hitting area of the barrel is sometimes marked on bats made for young players.)

5. When the bat makes contact with the ball, both your feet should be on the ground and *your hands should be in the* palm up, palm down *position* (the palm of your top hand is facing up and the palm of your bottom hand is facing down) (Figure 2-11).

6. As soon as you hit the ball, *snap your wrists so that your top wrist rolls over your bottom wrist*. It's very important to make this move at the right time. If you snap your wrists too early or too late, you'll lose power and you won't make a good hit.

7. *Follow through* (Figure 2-12) *by continuing the swing after you've hit the ball.* Some hitters bring the bat up high around their shoulder on the follow-through. Other hitters keep the bat lower. Use the follow-through that works best for you.

Being able to move your bat quickly is important. You only have less than a second to see the ball coming and decide where it will enter the strike zone. If you can move your bat very quickly, you will have more time to see where the ball is coming and it will be harder for the pitcher to fool you.

Getting Hit by the Ball

2-13

2-13: Practice getting out of the way of pitch by having a friend throw tennis balls at you. Roll the front shoulder in and keep the head tucked for protection.

Every new batter worries about getting hit with the ball. If you are afraid in the batter's box during a game, the pitcher will know it and use your fear against you, by throwing inside strikes. Before you know it, you'll be sitting back on the bench. The best way to get over your fear is to learn how to take a hit.

Take a Hit Drill

Have a teammate throw slow balls at you. Practice turning your back to the pitch and protecting you face and head (Figure 2-13). Once you learn how to protect yourself, your fear will go away. Getting hit with the ball does sting for a while, but the sting will wear off. Always wear a helmet while batting.

Make-Believe Drill

To practice your swing when you don't have anyone to pitch to you, take your bat outside and find some objects (such as a hole in a fence, a rock on the ground, a car parked down the street, a sign, or a leaf on a low tree branch). Face one of the objects and take your stance. Even though the object isn't close to you, and even though it doesn't move, pretend that it is the ball coming toward you, and swing at it. This drill helps you work on your batting style, and it helps you build up your batting muscles.

Hitting the Pitch

Only swing at balls that come through the strike zone (the area above home plate that is between your armpits and knee tops). If the pitcher misses the strike zone and you don't take a swing, it's a ball. Once you have four balls, you get to walk to first base.

The more you crouch in your stance, the smaller the strike zone becomes. Since the pitcher's target is smaller, he's more likely to throw balls. If you want to get a walk, make your strike zone smaller.

The straighter you stand, the bigger your strike zone becomes. Since the pitcher's target is bigger, he's more likely to throw through the zone. If you want to get a hit, make your strike zone bigger.

Timing (hitting the ball at the right spot in the strike zone) is very important to good hitting. Hit the ball at the point where it comes into the strike zone. If you hit the ball too early, it can bounce off the end of the bat. If you hit the ball too late (when it is deep in the strike zone), it will be harder to hit it with the barrel of your bat, and you'll probably miss the ball or hit a foul ball. Remember, you have to adjust your timing to the pitcher throwing on the mound (Figure 2-14).

2-14: It's important to pick up the pitch as quickly as possible. When a pitcher like fireball Roger Clemens is on the mound, you don't have a lot of time to recognize what type of pitch is coming.

Strike Zone Drill

Take your stance in the batter's box. Have the pitcher throw a variety of balls through your strike zone. Don't swing at them; instead, watch the pitches and have the catcher call each one as a strike or a ball. Keep up the drill until you are able to read each pitch correctly (Figure 2-15).

The pitcher's job is to strike you out. He doesn't throw straight through the strike zone. He throws high and low, inside and outside the strike zone. Here's the most common pitches and how to hit them:

The Inside Pitch

On an inside pitch, the ball crosses the plate on the inside of the plate (close to your body). Swing to make contact with the ball out in front of the plate. If you wait until the ball crosses the plate, your arms will be jammed up against your body and your swing won't have any power.

The Outside Pitch

On an outside pitch, the ball crosses the plate on the outside of the plate (away from your body). You can wait a bit longer to hit the ball and still make contact out in front of the plate.

2-15: The best way to improve your knowledge of the strike zone is to stand in the batter's box while a pitcher is throwing. Call each pitch out ("Ball, outside!") as they come in. Compare your opinion with the catcher's.

When you take your stance at the plate, what's going through your mind?

Every time I go up to the plate, my goal is to hit the ball hard somewhere, anywhere. If I do that, then I'm happy no matter what happens. Everybody would like to get a hit every time up, but with nine guys on the field with gloves, it's impossible.

What has helped you to win seven National League batting titles?

Well, the first thing is the amount of batting practice and hard work I do both before and during the season. I also think that I've had success because I stick to what I do best. I'm a contact hitter. I'm not a power hitter and I don't try to hit home runs. Hitting singles and doubles is my game and that's what I concentrate on perfecting.

Your career batting average is .334. How do you manage to stay away from big slumps?

First of all, every hitter on every level of baseball goes through slumps. Big league hitters fall into slumps all the time so don't feel bad if you find yourself in one.

When I get into a slump, I know through experience that eventually I will come out of it. In the meantime, I try to figure out what I'm doing wrong at the plate and work hard on correcting it. That way, the slumps don't last too long. Slumps happen to the best hitters in baseball. The key is to have confidence in yourself, and not panic.

What's one piece of advice you could give to a young hitter?

Always make sure you look for a good pitch to hit. Hitting can be very difficult and you'll make it a lot harder on yourself if you start swinging at bad pitches. If you get a good pitch, be aggressive and rip it. If it's not one you like, keep your patience and wait for a better one.

2-16, 2-17: Rafael Palmeiro takes a compact, level swing to rip a line drive to the outfield.

The Fast Ball

A *fastball* is one that is pitched hard and fast. If you think the pitcher is going to throw a fastball, take your stance near the back of the pitcher's box. This will give you more time to aim for the ball.

The Change-Up

After the pitcher has been pitching fastballs, he might pitch a slower ball to catch you off guard. Change-of-pace pitches, called *change-ups*, are hard to hit because they look like a fastball at first. If you think a slower pitch is coming, move forward in the box.

Terms for Batted Balls

2-18: When sacrifice bunting, pivot on the ball of your back foot and slide your top hand up to the barrel of the bat. Hold the barrel of the bat slightly higher than the handle, and push it out away from your body. Bend at the knees and lower your eyes so they're closer to the flight of the ball.

- **Grounder.** A ball that bounces or rolls on the ground.
- **Line Drive.** A ball that flies straight and low at least as far as the infielders before bouncing or being caught (Figures 2-16 and 2-17).
- **Fly Ball.** A ball that travels high in the air.
- **Sacrifice Fly.** A long fly ball that's caught for an out, but the runner on third base has time to run home for a score after the ball is caught.

Bunt

A *bunt* is when you choose to lay the ball down with the bat so it rolls a few feet into the infield. To bunt, use your regular stance, but when the pitcher throws the ball, move your feet so they point toward the pitcher. Hold the bat in front of your chest. Slide your top hand up the barrel of the bat and hide your fingers behind the bat so they won't get hit by the ball. Use the bat to drop the ball toward the ground so it will bounce into the infield.

2-19

Sacrifice Bunt

On a *sacrifice bunt* (Figure 2-18), you bunt hoping that a runner already on base can advance to the next base, even though you will be put out. If the runner is on third, bunt the ball toward first, so he can score while the pitcher or first baseman is getting the ball. When you make a sacrifice bunt you are giving up your turn at bat to help your team.

On a *base hit bunt* (Figure 2-19), you bunt hoping to make it to first. When you're bunting for a base hit, send the ball toward third and sprint as fast as you can for first.

2-19: When a left-handed hitter drag bunts, his momentum should be moving toward first base as he makes contact with the ball. Delino DeShields is already on his way to beating out a base hit.

Practice, Practice, Practice

Practice helps you make the most of your abilities. Practice your swing until you can swing the bat smoothly every time. If a certain kind of pitch gives you trouble, have a friend pitch it to you over and over and over. The more you practice, the better hitter you'll become (Figure 2-20).

Make It Up, Play It OUt

Here's a game you can play to practice hitting.

Pepper

You need three or more players, a bat, and a baseball. All the players, except one, get into a line. They are the pitchers. The leftover player is the batter. The batter stands about 20 feet away and faces the first pitcher in the line. The pitcher throws the ball to the batter, who tries to hit it back to him (the batter does not hit the ball very far or very hard). If the batter misses the ball, he goes to the end of the pitching line, and the pitcher that threw the ball becomes the batter. Keep playing until all the players have had a turn at bat.

2-20: The only way to become a great hitter is practice, practice, and more practice. Kirby Puckett was one of the best hitters in the major leagues during his career, and he took batting practice every day.

Keep Focused

1. To be a great hitter, you need to find your own style.
2. Place yourself in the batter's box so it's easy to swing the bat over home plate.
3. Always remember to see the ball when it leaves the pitcher's hand. Watch the ball all the way to your bat.
4. Take a stride toward the pitcher to put power into your swing.
5. Only swing at balls that come through the strike zone.
6. Hit the ball at the point where it comes into the strike zone.
7. Follow through after you've hit the ball.
8. To bunt, hold the bat in front of your chest. Slide your top hand up the barrel of the bat. Use the bat to drop the ball toward the ground.
9. Every time you step up to the plate, believe that you're going to get a hit.

CHAPTER 3

Running the Bases

You get a hit! You drop the bat, sprint all-out for first, and make a good turn. The left fielder fields the ball, but juggles it briefly. You take off for second base. He fires it to the second baseman. You hit the dirt. The second baseman receives the throw. You slide into the bag the instant before he tags you. You're safe!

To be a good base runner you have to be able to run fast, but a speedy sprint isn't everything. Your mind has to be speedy, too. You have to be aware of what's happening around you, and you have to make fast choices on when to run, when to slide, and in the higher levels of play, how far to take a lead, and when to steal. Knowing the right thing to do helps you stay alive (not get tagged out) on the basepaths and increases your chances of getting home safe for a score.

Rules and Terms for Runners

1. **The Path to First Base.** The foul line runs from home plate and through first base. Halfway between home plate and first base, another line begins. This line runs outside and parallel to the foul line. When you run

from home plate to first base, you have to run between these two lines or you'll be called out.

2. **Tagged Out at First.** When you're running to first base, you must touch the base before the fielder, who has the ball, tags (touches) it, or you're out.

3. **Tagged Out at Second, Third, and Home.** When you're advancing toward second, third, or home, and a defensive player tags you with the ball (or with the glove that has the ball in it), you're out.

4. **Forced to Run.** When there's a runner on first, or runners on first and second, or runners on first, second, and third, and a fair ball (except for a fly ball that's caught) is hit, a base runner is forced to move to the next base. A fielder can get the runner out by tagging the base ahead of the runner before he gets there.

5. **Avoiding the Tag.** If you run more than three feet from the foul line in order to keep from being tagged, you're out.

6. **Base Coaches.** The offensive team has a first-base coach and a third-base coach. They can help tell you when to run and when to stay on base.

Before You Step into the Batter's Box

Before you step into the batter's box, you should know the *game situation*, meaning the score, number of outs, inning, count, and number of men on the bases. (The count is explained later in this chapter.) Take a good look at the defense, and you might see things that will help you when it's time to run to first base (Figure 3-1). For example, if you notice before the pitch that the left fielder is playing *shallow* (close to the infield), then if you hit the ball solidly to left field, you'll know without even watching the ball that it's going over his head.

Breaking from Home Plate

When you're at bat, there are three ways to become a base runner:

1. **When you hit a fair ball.** A fair ball is any ball that lands on fair ground.

2. **When you hit the ball over the outfield fence.** This is an automatic home run, but you must touch all the bases in turn for it to count.

3. **When four balls are called.** In this case you walk to first base.

When you hit a fair ball, you want to get there as fast as you can. If you hit a grounder, don't waste any time watching the ball. *Drop* your bat (*never* throw it), and sprint for first base. You never know when an infielder will *bobble* (be unable to catch) a grounder and miss throwing to the base in time to put you out.

When you hit the ball out of the infield, keep your eyes on the ball as you *break* (start) for first. *Round* first base (tag it as you head to second) even if you don't think your hit is more than a single. A fumbled (dropped) ball by an outfielder could turn your single into a double. Here's how you round first base: Before you get to the base, move slightly away from the foul line (Figure 3-2). Turn toward second base and touch the inside of first base. Hit the *bag* (base) with either foot without breaking your stride (slowing down). This will keep you from making a too-wide turn (Figure 3-3). Run with your head up and keep your eyes on the

3-1: Before you dig into the batter's box, take a moment to re-think the game situation. Factors such as the inning, score, number of outs, or runners on base may have an influence on what you want to accomplish at the plate.

3-2, 3-3: If your hit makes it through the infield, make a gradual turn toward first base. Hit the bag without breaking stride and have your momentum going toward second base.

ball. If you lose sight of the ball, or aren't sure whether to keep going toward second, listen to the base coach.

Taking a Lead

When a runner is on base and he moves off toward the next base before the pitcher makes his pitch, it's called *taking a lead* (Figure 3-4). In youth baseball, runners don't take leads, but as you get older and play at the higher levels, you'll need to know how. Taking a lead is a way of shortening the distance to the next base. It can be risky because if the pitcher throws the ball to the baseman and he tags you before you can get back on base, you're out.

You have to be smart about how far away from base you can get when you take your lead (Figure 3-5). If you're on first, the length of your lead will depend on how quick you are and how good the pitcher's *pick-off move* (throw to the base) is. Make sure you can get back to the bag safely if the pitcher throws to the first baseman. When you are off the base, keep your weight on the balls of your feet, and your hands and arms, loose and hanging. Never cross you legs. If the pitcher *throws over* to first when your legs are crossed, you'll be slow getting back to the base.

When taking your lead, don't take your eyes off the pitcher. Once he starts his pitch, he can't throw over to the base, so shuffle a couple more steps off the bag to lengthen your lead and to get your momentum (motion) going toward second. If there's no play (hit or walk), get back to the bag fast.

When you're on second base, you can take a little longer lead. If the pitcher turns toward second, get back there. He may be faking, but it's better to play it safe. When he goes into his windup, shuffle a couple more steps toward third.

When you're on third base, make sure that you take your lead outside the baseline, in foul territory. If a ball hits you in fair territory, you're out. Take a lead off the base about the same distance that the third baseman is from the base. When the pitcher starts his windup, start walking toward home. If there's no play, get back to the bag in a hurry. A good catcher can throw you out if you're caught snoozing. Watch for *passed balls* (balls that get by the catcher) and *wild pitches* (pitches that are thrown so high or wide that they can't be caught by the catcher); they're sure to be runs if you're paying attention.

3-4, 3-5: When taking your lead, cross your left leg behind the right leg, bring the right leg over, and take two more shuffle steps. Don't ever cross your left leg over in front of you. You won't be able to get back to the bag on a quick pick-off throw. Always keep your eye on the pitcher, and pay attention to how far you're getting off the bag. You may be able to get a bigger lead the next time on base.

Running on a Hit

When you're on base and the ball is hit, keep your eyes on it. Don't run just because you hear the crack of the bat or you might get caught off base. On a fly ball, go about halfway. If the outfielder doesn't make the catch, you'll be ready to advance to the next base. If he does make the catch, you'll be able to get back to the base.

Advance to the next base if the runner ahead of you advances. Even if he has made a mistake and gets tagged out, you can take his place and your team will still have a runner on the base.

Tagging Up

When a fly ball is hit, the runner can try to *tag up* (move to the next base after the ball has been caught). When there's less than two outs and a fly ball is hit *deep* (far into the outfield), run back to the bag, keep one foot on it, and watch the play. When the ball is caught, push off the bag and sprint toward the next base. Be aware of the other base runners when tagging up. You don't want to break for the next base when the man ahead of you isn't advancing. Run on any fly ball when there are two outs.

Ground Balls

When a grounder is hit, you need a different kind of base-running. If you're on first, you must advance to the next base.

If you're on second or third and the bases behind you are full, you are forced to run. If you're not forced to run, only advance if you're sure you'll be safe.

Rundowns

A *rundown* is when you are caught between bases with a defensive player on each side of you and one of them has the ball. When you're caught in a rundown on a ground ball, make the rundown last as long as you can so other runners can advance while the defensive players are busy trying to tag you.

When you're on second base and a grounder is hit to your right, make sure it goes through the infield before you advance. If the ball is hit to your left, run for third. With a good lead you can usually beat the throw to third. If there's a man on first, you have to run anyway.

When you're the third base runner, break for home on nearly every ground ball. With a good lead, you should be able to beat out a throw from almost anywhere in the infield.

Bunts

When the batter bunts, make sure the ball is on the ground before you run. If the ball pops up, the catcher or pitcher can step up, make the catch, then tag you out for a double play.

Situation Baseball Drill

Have all nine players in their positions on the field. The remaining players should go to home plate as baserunners. With your coach hitting the balls out, practice running the bases as if it were a real game. Use smart judgment and show your speed on the basepaths.

3-6: Rickey Henderson has stolen more bases than anyone in the history of baseball. Stealing bases is not only about being fast, you have to be observant of the pitcher and defense, and have good instincts on the basepaths.

Stealing

When a runner tries to *steal* a base (Figure 3-6), he takes a long lead and sprints for the next base as the pitcher goes into his motion. If the runner reaches the next base before the defense tags him out, he's stolen that base. Bases are not stolen in youth baseball, but they are at higher levels of play.

A stolen base advances the runner to scoring position. It can take away the threat of a double play when first base is empty. Why aren't bases stolen all the time? Because stealing is risky. When a player tries to steal a base and fails, he's out, and his team loses a base runner.

Delayed Steal

The delayed steal is sometimes used in youth baseball. On a *delayed steal*, the base runner waits until the catcher throws the ball to the pitcher before breaking for the next base. It works best when the infielders have left the next base unguarded.

Double Steal

The *double steal* is when two base runners successfully steal bases on the same play.

One kind of double steal attempt is when there are runners on first and third. The runner on first tries a regular steal, a delayed steal, or fakes a steal in order to get the catcher to throw to second. When the throw is made to second, the runner on third steals home. The runner on third should see the ball go over the pitcher's head before going for the steal.

A Good Jump Is Important

Taking a lead and getting a good *jump* (break into your sprint) are very important when you're trying to steal a base. Watch the pitcher throughout the game and see if he makes any certain movements just before he throws to the plate. If you can learn to identify the instant he commits to (decides to go for) the throw, you can get the quickest jump. Watch the baseman as you run. Where he positions himself on the bag will tell you where the throw is coming, and you can plan your slide. Read on to learn about sliding.

Sliding

A *slide* is when a runner is sprinting to a base and drops down to the ground to slide the last few feet to the bag. A slide is also called, *hitting the dirt*. Slides are used to avoid a tag (the slide makes you a smaller target) or to allow a player to run to a base at full speed without over-running (going beyond) it. There are different kinds of slides. The two slides that are used most by young players are the hook slide and the straight-in slide.

Hook Slide

This slide is called the *hook* because the runner slides with his body away from the base and hooks the bag with his foot.

When you're running toward the bag, look at the baseman. If he's making the catch on the infield side of the base, you slide into the outfield side of the base. If he's making the catch on the outfield side of the bag, slide into the infield side.

A few feet from the base, kick your lead foot out in front of you toward the side of the bag. (If you're sliding into the left side of the bag, lead with your left foot. If you're sliding into the right side of the bag, lead with your right foot.) Land on your butt, dragging your back foot out to the side and use it to hook the bag as you slide by. Be ready to grab the bag with your hand. Sometimes your slide will carry your foot beyond the bag.

Straight-in Slide

The *straight-in slide* is also known as the *stand-up slide* (Figure 3-7). On this slide, land on your butt with one leg doubled up underneath you and the other leg stretched out in front of you to touch the bag as you slide into it. As you hit the bag, brace your lead foot against it, push with your other leg, and the force from your slide will carry you back up into a standing position.

Sliding Drill

This is a drill that should be saved for a rainy day. Find an open area where the grass is wet to practice your sliding. Take off your shoes and run for the bag full speed. Practice all the different slides you might use in a game situation.

3-7: This is an example of a straight-in slide. Land on your butt with your arms up in the air. Make sure you go into the bag with your lead leg and not the bent leg underneath.

Make It Up, Play It Out

Pickle is a great game for practicing how to keep from being tagged in a rundown.

Pickle

You need three players, a baseball, two gloves, a ball, and a playing area with two bases. Two players, one holding the ball, and both wearing gloves, stand at the bases and the runner stands in between them. The runner tries to get to one of the bases safely. If he does, he changes places with the baseman at that bag. Keep playing until all players have had several turns in the middle.

Outside the Lines

WHEN STEALING ISN'T STEALING

In the second game of the 1917 World Series, between the Chicago White Sox and the New York Giants, Red Farber, pitcher for the White Sox, was on second base. When New York pitcher, Pol Perrit, went into his windup, Faber broke for third base, which was already taken by his teammate, Buck Weaver. After Faber made a dramatic head-first slide to third, Weaver looked down at him and asked Faber where he thought he was going. Faber looked up and said, "Back to pitch."

Keep Focused

1. Before you step into the batter's box, know the game situation.
2. When you hit a fair ball, sprint for first base as fast as you can.
3. When taking your lead, don't take your eyes off the pitcher.
4. When you're on third base, make sure you take your lead outside the baseline in foul territory.
5. On a fly ball, don't move so far from the bag that you can't get back safely if the fly ball's not a hit.
6. When a fly ball is hit, try to tag up after it's caught.
7. When you're caught in a rundown on a ground ball, make the rundown last as long as you can.
8. When you're on third, break for home on nearly every grounder.
9. When sliding, use the hook slide unless you need to get back up very fast. Then use the straight-in slide.

4

The Pitcher

Every play starts with a pitched ball. If you're the pitcher for your team, you're a very important member of your team's defense. Your job is to keep the other team from scoring by causing the batter to hit a ball that can be fielded for a putout, or by causing him to strike out.

Learning to pitch takes a lot of practice. Great pitchers all have their own style of pitching. The best way for you to find your pitching style is to learn the basics of pitching, then use them in a way that feels natural to you. The basics include: the grip, stance, windup, delivery, and follow-through.

On the Pitcher's Mound

The pitcher's mound is 18 feet in diameter and 10 inches above the level of the field. There are two positions that young players use on the mound: the windup position and the set position.

Windup Position

If you're a right-handed pitcher, stand behind the rubber and face the batter. Place your right foot on the rubber. Place your left foot about four or five inches behind the rubber. If you are a left-handed pitcher, your left foot is on the rubber and your right foot is back. (It's also okay for a pitcher to stand with both feet on the rubber.) Lean forward a little, letting your arms hang down in front of you. Keep the ball hidden inside your glove with your throwing hand. Shift your weight to your back foot and swing both arms down and back. Then swing both arms straight up above your head, bringing the ball behind the glove again. Pause for a second, then bring your throwing hand back as you stride forward with your back foot and turn your left side (for righties) or right side (for lefties) toward the batter. Bring your pitching arm forward and as you release the ball, turn your body so your chest is facing the batter. Follow through by continuing your arm motion and bringing your back foot forward to keep your balance.

Use the windup position (Figure 4-1) when there are no runners on base, because in the windup position, your windup takes longer than in the set position.

4-1: With no runners on base, the pitcher can throw to the plate from the windup position.

Set Position

If you're a right-handed pitcher, stand in front of the rubber, and face third base. If you're a left-handed pitcher, face first base. Place the outside edge of your back foot (right for righties, left for lefties) against the front edge of the rubber. (Don't stand on the rubber or you'll slip when you pitch.) Your front foot should be four or five inches closer to the front of the mound (both feet should be pointing toward third base for righties and first base for lefties). As you bring your throwing arm back, pick up your front foot and take a short stride toward home plate. Turn your chest toward the batter as your throwing arm moves forward and releases the ball. After the ball is released, follow through by continuing your arm motion and bringing your back foot forward to keep your balance.

Use the set position when there's a runner on base, because in the set position, your windup takes very little time.

The Delivery

There are two ways for a young pitcher to *deliver* (release) the ball: The three-quarters, overhand delivery, and the sidearm delivery.

Three-Quarters, Overhand Delivery

Overhand delivery means that the pitcher's arm is above his shoulder when he pitches the ball. On the *three-quarters* (Figure

4-2), overhand delivery, the ball is released when it is just in front of your head or ear. This is the most popular delivery for young players because it gives you speed on the ball.

Sidearm Delivery

On the *sidearm* delivery (Figure 4-3), your pitching arm is out to the side of your body and the ball is released at the height of your ribs. The sidearm delivery is hard to hit. To a right-handed batter, the sidearm pitch looks like it's coming into the strike zone from behind him. The ball has some up and down movement during flight, but won't break from side to side. Young players usually use the three-quarters overhand delivery, but if throwing sidearm happens to feel right to you, go for it.

There are two other deliveries that are used by some professional ball players. They are:

Full, Overhand Delivery

On the *full*, overhand delivery, the ball is released when the arm is straight up in the air (like the position of the 12 on a clock). When the ball is released from this position, the pitch tends to fly straight. The ball may have some up and down movement during flight, but it won't break from side to side. Since side-to-side movement is important to most pitches, the full overhand delivery isn't used very often. Young players shouldn't use this delivery because it's very hard on the pitching arm and can easily cause an injury. Leave this pitch to the pros.

4-2: The release point from the pitcher can vary from straight over the top to three-quarter armed delivery to sidearmed. Here Todd Stottlemyer throws a three-quarter armed fastball.

Kinds of Pitches

The Fastball

The *fastball* (Figure 4-4), also called the *hummer*, is your most important pitch. It's thrown hard and fast, and works well against the batter because of its speed and action (movement). When a pitcher throws a fastball, he puts *spin* on it. Spin means that the ball turns while it's in flight. Spin helps the ball travel faster and causes the ball to break up or down while in flight. The break can cause the batter to change the level of his bat in mid-swing, and he's likely to hit the ball with less power or not hit it at all.

4-3: It's very difficult to pick up pitches from pitcher Brad Clontz because he throws all of his pitches sidearm.

The Sinking Fastball

The *sinking fastball* is a fastball that breaks downward during flight. It's a great pitch to use when you want the batter to hit a

4-4: This is a grip for a straight fastball. It's held across the seams, and gives the pitcher his best velocity. The palm should face the hitter when the ball is released.

4-5: Here is a grip for an overhand breaking ball. Notice how the hand is turned in toward the batter. Make sure you consult with your coach before attempting to throw this pitch.

ground ball. Because the pitch comes in low, the batter will most likely have to use the lower half of his bat, which usually sends the ball on the ground to the infield.

Grip the ball with your thumb underneath, and across the seam. Your first two fingers are over the top of the ball, resting along the narrow seams. The ball will sink when it breaks because the spinning seams stay on the sides of the ball as it travels and do not resist the air.

Release the ball when your arm is just in front of your head or ear, and put pressure on it with your index finger, which helps it to sink.

The Change-Up

After you've thrown a few fastballs, the batter will be expecting them, so you might want to change to a slower ball in order to throw off his swing. A *change-up* pitch looks like a fastball but is much slower. To throw the change-up, make your delivery like that of a fastball, only throw the ball slower.

The grips used to throw the change-up keeps your index finger to the side of the ball, giving the ball less power, and making it travel slower. The *OK grip* is the easiest to control. It's called the OK because when you make the grip your hand looks like it's making the sign for OK. Fold your thumb and index finger in the shape of an O. Your other three fingers stand up, making the K. Place the ball deep in your palm, with one side tight against the O. When you lay your top fingers over the ball, your middle and ring fingers should be a little off to the side of the two narrow seams. Grip the ball with the undersides of your fingers instead of with your fingertips.

All change-ups are thrown much slower than a fastball, but you still want to throw your change-ups at different speeds. For example, if your fastball flies at 90 mph (miles per hour), one change-up pitch might fly at 80 mph, another at 70 mph, and another at 65 mph.

Other Kinds of Pitches

There are other kinds of pitches that are used by older and more experienced pitchers. They are listed here so you know what they are. These pitches should never be tried by a young pitcher because they use a twisting motion that can cause bad injury to the bones and ligaments of a young arm. Young pitchers who use these pitches will ruin their arm for playing baseball. Save them until you're grown, then learn them from an expert.

Breaking Pitches

Breaking pitches (Figure 4-5) break differently than the fastball, depending on how the spin is put on the ball and how it's thrown. Some breaking pitches can look like a fastball at first, which may confuse the batter.

- *The Curveball.* A right-handed curveball breaks from the pitcher's right to his left as he faces the batter (Figure 4-6). A left-handed curveball breaks from the pitcher's left to his right as he faces the batter. If the batter is expecting a fastball, the break of the curveball can fool him into altering his swing.

- *The Slider.* The slider looks like a fastball until it gets three or four feet in front of the batter, then it appears to break slightly, making it very hard for the batter to hit the ball with the barrel of the bat.

4-6: Tom Gordon is throwing a curveball in this picture. Notice the ball has a slight arc coming out of his hand. This delays the speed of the pitch and can affect the hitter's timing.

Aiming Your Pitches

Look at the strike zone when you begin your windup. Keep your eyes on the strike zone until the ball has been released. It takes a lot of practice for you to learn how to pitch the ball through the strike zone. The following drills can help.

Aiming Drill with a Batter

Practice pitching the ball to the catcher with a batter standing at the plate like he's ready to hit (Figure 4-7). The batter doesn't strike at the ball, he just stands there in hitting position so you can get used to pitching through his strike zone. When you throw to the catcher, have him call out a ball if you're outside the strike zone, or call out a strike if your pitch passes through the strike zone. Have the batter take a turn standing on both sides of the plate.

4-7: Spend your practice time from the mound with a hitter in the batter's box. It creates a more game-like situation, and the batter can offer his opinions and observations.

Aiming Drill without a Batter

Use chalk to draw a strike zone on a wall. Make the zone about 17 inches wide and 24 inches high. Pitch the ball at the zone from about 20 feet away. Pitch the ball at the zone over and over until you can hit it almost every time. Then use the chalk to divide the zone into four equal parts.

Practice pitching the ball at the different areas of the zone. Once you are good at hitting all the areas of the zone, throw your pitches from farther away.

Practice these drills until you can aim your pitches at the top, bottom, inside (near the batter), outside (away from the batter), and corners of the strike zone.

When you pitch to a batter, it's you against him. Don't worry so much about trying to strike him out. The only time you want to work for a strikeout is when a run will be scored unless he strikes out. Work to make the batter hit the ball in such a way that the fielders can make a putout. Here are some strategies to help you (Figure 4-8):

4-8: What you throw and where you throw it is very important, but don't forget to finish all of your pitches. Follow through after every pitch to achieve your best results.

Pitch Away from the Center of the Strike Zone

The best way for a batter to get a hit is to hit the ball on the sweet spot of the bat. Send your pitches through the strike zone away from the center of the plate. This may cause the batter to hit the ball near the top or near the handle of the bat, making a putout more likely.

Mix Up Your Pitches

If you throw only fastballs, the batter will learn to judge the speed of the ball and be better able to hit your pitches. Throw a few fastballs, then switch to the change-up. The batter will think a fastball is coming, but because it takes longer for the change-up to get to the plate, he might swing too soon. Mix up the rising fastball, sinking fastball, and the change-up. Throw the change-up at different speeds. Mixing up your pitches can mix-up the batter.

Watch Where the Batter Stands in the Box

Watch the batter carefully as he stands in the box. If he's near the back of the box, he's expecting a fastball. Throw him a slower, outside pitch. If he's standing near the front of the batter's box, he's expecting a slower pitch. Throw him an inside fastball.

When You're Ahead of the Count

The *count* is the number of balls and strikes on the batter. Balls are counted first, then strikes. A count of two and one, means the batter has two balls and one strike. The count of three and two, (the batter has three balls and two strikes) is also known as a *full count*, meaning that if there is one more strike, the batter is out, or if there is one more ball, he walks to first base.

Getting ahead of the count means that there are more strikes than balls. If the batter has already used up two strikes, and you pitch through the strike zone, he has to make contact with the ball or he strikes out. This is a good time to give him a pitch that he can't hit well.

When You're Behind the Count

When you're behind the count, meaning that there are more balls than strikes, go with your best pitch, which should be your fastball. You should be confident that you can throw your fastball for a strike.

Get to Know the Batter

Getting to know the batter doesn't mean taking him to lunch. It means watching him when he's at bat, remembering how he batted the last time you came up against him, or asking other players about him. Watch the other team's batters whenever you are sitting on the bench. If you know the batter's strengths and weaknesses, you can use them against him. For example, don't throw a change-up to a poor hitter. If your fastball is too fast for him, keep using it, because a change-up will probably be just his speed.

Outside the Lines

WHAT'S THE BIG K?
A strikeout is also called the big K. The "K" comes from the letter, "k," in the word "strike."

Strategy Against the Runners

If there's a runner on base, it's the pitcher's job to keep him close to the base so he can't steal a base or run two bases on a hit. If you're playing at a level where bases are stolen, the best way to keep the runner close to the base is to decide how far you will allow him to move when he takes his lead. If he crosses that point before you start your windup, throw to the side of the base he is on. Make the throw at knee level so it will be easy for the infielder to catch.

Make your windup longer sometimes and shorter other times. By changing the length of your windup, the runner won't be able to guess how much time he has to move back to the base.

You're a Fielder, Too

You're not just a pitcher. As soon as you release your pitch, you become a fielder. A pitcher has a lot of fielding jobs to do. Here's some of the most important ones:

- **Catching Balls Hit Back at You.** When hit balls and bunts come back at you, charge the ball, keep it in front of you, bend down, and scoop the ball up in both hands. Then fire the ball to the base. Make sure you give the fielder enough time to get to the base before you make your throw.

  If you throw to first, throw the ball to the second-base side of the bag, out of the way of the incoming runner.

  If it's a double-play and the shortstop is covering second, throw the ball a step in front of second base on the third-base side so he can catch it, hit the bag, and get out of the way of the runner for the throw to first. Do the same thing for the second baseman, but lead him a step off the bag on the first-base side.

- **Backing up the Bases.** Be ready to run to first base or home plate to catch a ball fielded by the first baseman or the catcher in order to put out the runner.

4-9: With a runner on first base, you now have two offensive players to worry about. Pitching from the stretch, you should throw over to first on occasion to keep the runner close.

Move It Off the Mound on Every Hit

Even if looks like you won't be needed on the play, move off the mound so you are ready to back up a base or call the play. If the ball is hit toward first base, move in that direction. If your first baseman is fielding, you are already on your way to cover the bag (Figure 4-10). Run toward the bag parallel to the baseline so you won't crash into the runner. The first baseman should get the ball to you before you get to the bag. That way, you can catch the ball, tag the bag, and be ready to throw to another base if needed.

Rules for Pitchers

Some important rules for pitchers are:
1. Pitchers are not allowed to rub the ball on themselves, their glove, or their uniform.

2. Pitchers are not allowed to change the surface of the ball. This includes making the ball rough, or adding things like spit, wax, mud, or gum.

3. Pitchers are not allowed to hit the batter with the ball on purpose (called a bean ball).

4. The batter must be in the batter's box, in a position to take a swing before the ball is pitched.

5. Pitchers are not allowed to balk once they've started their windup. Some of the ways a pitcher can balk are: starting the windup, then faking a throw to first base; throwing to any base without first stepping toward that base; faking a pitch to the batter, then throwing to a base; or dropping the ball, even if it's an accident.

4-10: On ground balls that are hit to the first base side, it's the pitcher's responsibility to cover the bag. The first baseman may not have time to get back to make the putout.

Working with the Catcher

The pitcher and catcher work together as partners. They need to think alike and know what to expect from each other. Spend some time before each game talking with the catcher about the batters and what strategies you will use. The catcher should know what your best pitches are. When you are on the mound, the catcher signals the pitches to you. Most batteries use a number system to keep things simple. A common number system is: one finger means a fastball, two fingers mean a curveball, and three fingers mean a change-up. (Remember that young players won't be using a curveball. You, your pitcher, and your coaches will work out your own number system.)

Taking Care of Your Arm

It's important to take good care of your pitching arm. If it's injured, you can't play. The best way to keep your arm from being hurt is to warm up before starting a game. Jog slowly until you begin to sweat. Then stretch your whole body (you can use the stretches in Chapter 1). Make some warm-up throws and keep them nice and easy.

When you're on the bench between innings, keep a jacket on your arm. Even in warm weather, a cool breeze can make your muscles stiff. Never pitch with a sore arm.

Make It Up, Play It Out

Target

You need a target. Things that make a good target are an archery target, a tire swing, or a paper target stuck to the trunk of a tree. Players take turns pitching the ball at the target. If the pitch hits the center of the target, it's worth three points. If it hits the edge of the target, it's worth two points. If it just misses the target, it's worth one point. The first player to get 15 points, wins the game. The first time you play the game, stand about 20 feet from the target. When you're an expert at hitting the target from 20 feet, increase your distance.

1. Your pitching style includes: the grip, stance, windup, delivery, and follow-through. Experiment with them until you find the style that's right for you.
2. Two positions to use on the pitcher's mound are the set position and the windup position. When there's a runner on base, use the set position.
4. The fastball, or hummer, is your most important pitch.
5. Mix up your pitches to keep the batter off balance.
6. To keep the batter from hitting the ball hard, pitch away from the center of the strike zone.
7. Watch where the batter stands in the box. If he's near the back, he's expecting a fastball, so throw a slower, outside pitch. If he's standing near the plate, he's expecting a slower pitch, so throw a fastball.
8. Once you've pitched the ball, be ready to catch balls hit back to you.
9. Move off the mound on every hit, even if it looks like you won't be needed on the play.
10. Work with your catcher. The two of you should think alike and know what to expect from each other.

5

The Catcher

When you're the catcher, you're on the receiving end of around 120 fast pitches in every game, and you have to be able to catch every one of them. That takes good catching ability, and a lot of practice.

The catcher is one half of that very special team, the battery. The other half is the pitcher. On every single pitch, the catcher watches the batter, gets a feel for his pitcher, and decides which pitch will keep the other team from scoring. The catcher must be a smart leader. His pitcher and his other teammates depend on him to make the right decisions. Catching ability, courage, smarts, and leadership—if you've got all four, you just might make a great catcher.

Catcher's Gear

Because catchers sometimes get hit by the ball or another player, they wear special equipment that helps protect them from injury. A mask protects the head, a padded chest protector covers the chest, and shin guards protect the knees and lower legs.

The catcher's mitt is shaped to help you catch the ball. It also protects your hands from foul balls and swinging bats.

The best way to wear your mitt is with the heel of your non-throwing hand slightly out of the base of the mitt. If your hand is all the way into the mitt, it's hard to turn your wrist.

Catcher's Stance

A catcher needs the correct stance behind the plate in order to do his job well. The correct stance is rock-solid, well-balanced, and controlled. It gives you the ability to handle any kind of pitch, even one in the dirt, and still lets you spring up for throwing to the bases. If you're not sure where to take your stance, stand behind the plate and the batter. Put one arm straight out in front of you. Move close enough to the batter so you can touch his back shoulder with your fingers. If you are any closer to the batter, you're more likely to get hit by the bat as the batter drops it to run.

5-1: The chair stance puts the catcher in the best possible position to do his job. It allows him to shift his body to handle high, low, inside, and outside pitches. A catcher can also drop to his knees in this position if the ball is thrown in the dirt.

Chair Stance

Crouch down with your legs, wide apart and your feet, flat on the ground. Shift your weight forward onto the balls of your feet You should look like you're just about to sit down in a chair (Figure 5-1). This low, wide base helps you keep your balance and makes you a good target for the pitcher. Bend your elbows and bring your hands up in front of you, but not so far up that they block your view of the pitcher. Keep your throwing hand on the back of your glove or behind you to protect it. Keep your head straight ahead, so it's protected by your mask. (There is no protection on the sides of the mask.) It's natural to want to shut your eyes when the batter swings, but keep them open so you can see the ball. You should be able to shift your body in all directions without losing your balance.

In the chair stance, you are ready to catch low, high, inside, or outside pitches. You're also ready to pop up to throw the ball as soon as you catch it.

The chair stance will take some getting used to, as your legs won't be strong enough at first to stay in this position very long. Over time, and with practice, they will get stronger and you will be able to last longer in the position.

Chair Stance Drill

You can help your legs get into shape for the chair stance by assuming the stance several times a day. Hold the stance until your legs feel tired, then stand back up. Work to increase the amount of time you can stay in the stance.

Squat Stance

Between pitches you can go into the squat stance to give you a bit of a rest, while still being ready to catch the ball. Bring one foot back a bit for balance and squat down so your butt rests on your heels. Balance your elbows on your knees and keep your mitt forward as a target for the pitcher. Remember to keep your throwing hand behind the mitt. Some young players kneel between pitches instead of using the squat stance.

Protect Your Throwing Hand

Always remember to keep your throwing hand behind or on the back of your mitt when catching the ball. You can fold your fingers into a fist behind the mitt, then open them as soon as you make the catch, or you can keep the back of your hand turned toward the pitcher. This way, if your fingers get hit by the ball, they'll bend forward. If your hand is turned the other way and gets hit, your fingers will bend backward and they could get broken or sprained.

Signaling the Pitch

Before the play begins, give your pitcher the signal for the pitch you want him to throw. Most batteries use a number system to keep things simple. A common number system is: one finger means a fastball, two fingers mean a curveball, and three fingers mean a change-up. (Remember that young players won't be using a curveball. You, your pitcher, and your coaches will work out your own number system.)

Use the fingers of your throwing hand to show the pitcher the number (Figure 5-2). Move your mitt to the side, rest your throwing elbow on your knee, and let your wrist hang down with your hand in a fist. Unfold the right number of fingers from the fist, letting them point toward the ground. Your pitcher can signal back that he'd like a different pitch, for example, by touching his hat.

Keep Your Body in the Path of the Ball

When receiving the pitch, always *keep your body in the path of the ball*. Let the pitch come to you instead of reaching for it. If

5-2: Hold your signal up against your uniform pants so the pitcher can pick it up easily. Put your finger(s) down slightly toward the right leg so they're hidden from the first base coach and/or runner.

5-3: If the pitch is in the dirt, the catcher should drop to his knees and block the ball with his body. Don't try to snare the ball with your glove because if the ball gets through, the runners on base will advance. Get in front of the ball and act as a backstop.

you stick your glove out to catch a pitch, your body is no longer in front of the ball and it's more likely to get *passed*. A passed ball is one that the catcher fails to stop.

Keep your body in front of the pitch by *swaying* (shifting your hips, legs, and upper body). Keep your feet still unless the pitch is so far outside or inside the strike zone that you can't reach it. If it's off to either side, shuffle a step to the right or to the left to get in front of it. If it's really far out of the strike zone, you may have to shuffle both feet in order to get your body in front of the ball.

When you sway with your body, hold your arms still and use the sway of your body to move them into position to catch the ball. This way, your arms do not appear to move to the umpire. When the ball just misses the strike zone and the umpire doesn't see your arms move to catch it, he may think that the ball did go through the strike zone and call a strike instead of a ball.

Wall the Ball on a Low Pitch

When a ball comes in very low, it's best to block it rather than reach for it (Figure 5-3). If you try to reach out and grab a ball in the dirt, your body is no longer in front of the ball, so there's nothing stopping it if you miss it with your glove. *Wall* the ball. Shift your body so you're in front of the ball and drop to your knees. Put your hands between your knees with your bare hand behind the mitt. Keep your palms up and your thumbs out. Keep your arms tight against your body to protect your elbows and to make a more solid wall. To keep the ball from running up your chest and getting away, form your body into a cup by rolling your shoulders forward.

Wild Pitch Drill

Put the catcher's gear on and have a teammate throw balls at you. (You can use tennis balls for this drill.) Make sure he mixes up the spots in which he's throwing the ball. Have him throw high balls, balls in the dirt, some way outside and others inside. Do whatever it takes to stop that ball from getting by you.

The Catcher's Arm

The catcher's arm is a powerful defensive weapon. Catchers can make big plays by throwing to kill a steal or by picking off daring runners. A catcher's reputation is another good weapon. If the runner knows that you have a strong arm, he might decide not to even try to steal.

Being able to throw well from the plate takes more than just a strong arm (Figure 5-4). You need to get into throwing posi-tion, fast. When you see the runner break for the base, don't waste time coming all the way out of your crouch. Stay low and keep the mitt close to your body so you can get the ball out of your mitt quickly. As you move to make the catch, get clear of the batter, take a step toward the base you are throwing to, aim at a spot low on the baseman's body, and throw.

5-4: A quick release is very important in the catcher's position. Get the ball out of your glove and bring it straight back behind your ear. *Do not drop your arm down to your side. It takes too long.* A short delivery is critical in attempting to throw out baserunners.

Catcher's Plays

Catching Pop Flies

When a batter pops the ball straight up in the air, above, to the right, or to the left of the batter's box, you should try to catch it. (If the popped ball is going toward the pitcher, let the third baseman or first baseman get it.)

To catch a popped ball, watch where the ball goes. Throw your mask away from where you want to make the catch, get under the ball, and wait for it (Figure 5-5). Hold your mitt, pocket side up. As soon as the ball is in the mitt, cover it with your free hand to keep it from popping back out. The reason for throwing the mask is because you can't see very well to the side or straight up with it on. When you throw the mask, throw it where you won't trip on it or where it won't hit anybody.

Pick Offs

A *pick off* is when a catcher makes a sudden throw to a base to catch a runner while he's off the base. A catcher with a strong, quick throw is able to pick runners off of all three bases as well as put out runners trying to steal second or third. If you notice that a runner is taking a long lead that leaves him open to getting caught off base, consider picking him off. A runner who doesn't hurry back to the base after the pitch, or who doesn't keep his eye on the ball is also a possibility for a pick off play. To make a pick off play, signal the baseman and make sure he signals back, so you know he's seen the signal and knows you're throwing to him after the next pitch. To help you make your pick off move even faster, signal the pitcher to put the ball in a certain place. For example, if you're trying to pick a man off first, have the pitcher throw the ball to your right so you can step up, catch it and make the throw.

5-5: Find the ball immediately when the ball is popped up, and then throw your mask out of the way. Get to the spot where the ball is coming down. If you're facing the infield, take two steps forward to catch the ball. If your back is turned to the infield, take two steps backward. The reason for this is that the ball is hit with backspin and will carry a little toward the infield.

The Tag at the Plate

The play at the plate is one of the most exciting parts of the game. The runner is charging for home. He slides. Will he be safe? Or will you tag him out?

Who has influenced your career?

From when I was a kid growing up to now playing with the Boston Red Sox, there have been countless people who have helped me along the way. I had a great experience playing college ball at Seton Hall University. When I became a professional, Mike Easler helped me a lot with my hitting.

But I think my dad has had the greatest influence on me. He taught me to work hard at not just being a good player, but to be a good person as well.

The best pitchers in the major leagues are always trying their hardest to get you out. Do any of them ever scare you?

When you're facing a tough pitcher, whether it be Randy Johnson in the big leagues or the best pitcher in your little league, you should always remember one thing. Once the ball leaves his hand, it's just you against the ball. Don't worry about the pitcher's name or reputation, it's the ball you're competing against. Forget about who's throwing it, just swing the bat hard and whack it.

What have you learned since becoming a star in the major leagues?

Now that I've experienced some success as a hitter, I've noticed that most pitchers try to keep the ball away from me (on the outside corner) all the time. In order for me to keep producing, I had to learn to hit the outside pitch to the opposite field. Once I proved I could hit that pitch well, then they had to start pitching me inside again and the fielders now aren't sure how to defend me.

What advice would have for a young ballplayer?

I think young hitters should just try to do what they're best at. If you hit singles, work on being a contact hitter. If you can hit for power, practice driving the ball to the outfield. No two hitters are alike and youngsters shouldn't try to hit like someone they're not. Just be yourself.

5-6: Adjust your foot positioning to where the fielder throws the ball. Hold the ball in your glove with both hands when you tag the runner to make sure it doesn't jar loose.

Put your left heel on the middle of the front of the plate (this gives the runner a part of the plate to slide into so he doesn't crash into you). Start with your glove down and move it up to the ball when it comes to you from the field. This will help keep the ball in your glove. Make the catch and use your throwing hand to squeeze the ball into your mitt. Keep both hands on the ball for the rest of the play (Figure 5-6). Once you have the ball in both hands, move your left foot to the left corner of the plate and drop down on your right knee. You want to make the tag from the side of the plate. Your left leg will help protect you against the spikes of the runner's shoe. As the runner slides to the base, shift your weight forward to put some force behind the tag, then push the ball and the back side of your mitt against the lower part of the runner's leg.

If the runner slams into you, don't try to be a solid wall. Roll with the impact. This will help you hang on to the ball and make it less likely that you'll be injured.

Forced to Run Home

When the bases are *loaded*, meaning there are runners on first, second, and third, and a fair ball is hit, the runner on third is forced to run home.Position your foot on the right corner of the plate and get your glove up for the throw to home (Figure 5-7). You should be out of the way of the runner and facing the thrower. If there is the chance for a double play, position yourself two to three feet behind the plate before receiving the throw. Step into the throw and sweep your foot across the plate for the tag. This way you'll already be in motion for your throw to another base.

5-7: Put your right foot on home plate and stretch for the throw with your left leg. This will put you in a good position to throw to first base after receiving the ball if there's still a play.

Bunts

Field bunts that are close to the plate. When you think the batter's going to bunt, signal the pitcher and the infield to watch for a bunt. Get ready by standing a little higher in your stance with your right foot farther back than your left. This stance will help you get up and going toward the ball faster. Once the ball is hit and you have decided to go for it, flip off your mask and drop it behind you. Approach the ball on an angle, which helps you get your throw off much quicker. Use both your mitt and throwing hand to field the ball.

If you're not in the best position to field the bunt, direct your teammates. For example, if the third baseman and the pitcher are both charging the ball, call one of them off. Once the bunt is fielded by one of your teammates, tell him where the play is.

Working with the Pitcher

Work with the pitcher before the game to make a plan. Talk about the batters you'll face. Find out what you can about them. Have you gone up against them before? If so, what were their strengths and weaknesses? Use pitches that you know the batter has trouble hitting. Don't use pitches that he's good at hitting.

After the game has started, watch the batters closely. See how each batter handles different pitches and different areas of the strike zone. You should also keep track of the game situation and call pitches that might give your team an edge. For example, if there's a man on first, you might want to keep the pitches low in hopes of making the batter hit into a double play.

Give Your Pitcher Confidence

As a good leader, help your pitcher have confidence in his own abilities. Know his pitching style so you can recognize when something is wrong. Know his worst and best pitches, and what he likes and doesn't like to throw in different situations. Just as important, know his personality. Be able to recognize when he's losing his confidence or his temper. When your pitcher is losing his confidence, call for his best pitch until he gets his confidence back. When he's losing his cool, go out to the mound and talk to him (Figure 5-8). This will give him a chance to calm down. If you can keep him confident, he'll pitch his best, and he'll learn to trust you.

5-8: It's very important that the pitcher and catcher work well together. They should always communicate with each other and discuss their strategies. It's often the catcher's job to calm the pitcher down and give him confidence.

Make It Up, Play It Out

Stoop Ball

Stoop ball is a game for one player. You need a tennis ball or a hard, rubber ball (baseballs don't bounce well), and some steps (the stoop). Stand in front of the steps. Throw the ball against the steps and catch it when it bounces off them. If the ball hits the edge of a step, and you catch it on the fly, give yourself 10 points. If it hits the rising part of a step and is caught on the fly, give yourself one point. If the ball hits the flat part of a step, or is not caught on the fly, give the stoop one point. See if you can get to 100 points before the stoop does.

Keep Focused

1. The catcher must be a strong, smart leader.
2. Wear your mitt with the heel of your hand slightly out of the base of the mitt.
3. Use the chair stance during the pitch, and drop into the squat or onto your knees between pitches.
4. Stand in front of the plate after the ball is hit and be ready to receive a throw to the plate.
5. Always protect your throwing hand by keeping it on the back of your mitt.
6. When receiving a pitch, frame the plate and keep your body in front of the ball.
7. When a ball comes in very low, block it with your glove and scoop it up with your other hand.
8. To catch a popped ball, watch to see where the ball will come down, throw your mask, get under the ball, and wait for it.
9. If you're certain that the runner is going to steal on the next pitch, call a pitchout.
10. Make the tag at the plate from the side of the plate.

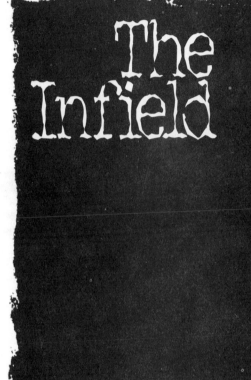

CHAPTER 6

The Infield

The *infield* refers to the territory that includes the four bases at the corners of the diamond and the area inside the diamond. The infield also refers to the four infield players: the first baseman, second baseman, shortstop, and third baseman. The infielders are a big part of your team's defense. It's their job to stop the other team from scoring by making putouts. To do their job, the infielders must be able to catch balls hit by the batter or thrown to them from a teammate. They must be able to throw fast and accurately. The infield is where most of the action is during a game.

The Infield

The territories covered by the members of the infield are:

- The *first baseman* covers first base and the area around it.
- The *second baseman* covers second base and the area from second base toward first base.
- The *shortstop* also covers second base and an area between second and third base.
- The *third baseman* covers third base and the area around it.

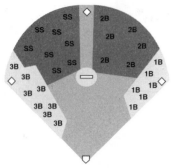

This diagram shows the area each position player is responsible for in the infield.

Putouts

When you play in the infield, you are always looking to make a putout (send a batter or runner back to the bench). There are three ways that infielders can make a putout. The first is by catching a batted ball before it touches the ground. The second is by tagging a runner with the ball or with the glove that has the ball in it when he's not on base. The third is, when you have the ball, to tag the bag at first before the runner gets there, or to tag the bag at another base on a force play. (There's more about the force play later in this chapter.)

Fielding Balls Hit to the Infield

Ready Position

No matter where you are positioned in the infield, you must always be *ready* to catch the ball (Figure 6-1). Being ready means two things: that you're watching the ball and that you're in the correct stance. To get into the ready stance, bend your knees, get up on the balls of your feet, and get your glove down near the ground. Now you're ready to move to receive the ball.

Reading the Pitch

Reading the pitch means guessing where the ball will go before it's hit. Here's how to guess: If a right-handed batter is up, begin moving to the left on an outside pitch and to the right on an inside pitch. If a left-handed batter is up, begin moving to the right on an outside pitch and to the left on an inside pitch. This is because most batters will tend to *push* (send the ball to their right) an outside pitch and *pull* (send the ball to their left) an inside pitch.

Off-speed pitches usually cause the batter to pull the ball. As soon as the pitcher releases the ball, move to the left or right, according to where you expect the ball to be hit.

Ground Balls and Bunts

When a ball is hit on the ground, your first job is to stop it. If you have time, charge (run toward) the ball. Don't wait for it to take a bad hop. Field it quickly and get rid of it. Try to get your body in front of it, get your glove down low, and, if the ball is on the ground, use both hands to scoop it into your glove (Figure 6-2).

6-1: An infielder should always be in good position to field the ball. Flex the knees a bit, bend at the waist, and reach out with your glove hand. Spread your feet apart wide to give yourself a broad base which will enable you to get low to the ground.

Soft Hands Drill

Practice fielding grounders without a glove. Have a teammate roll you the ball and field it in good position with your bare glove hand. This will force you to reach for the ball, keep your hand low to the ground, and "give" with the ball as you catch it.

Pop Flies

On a pop fly, locate the ball, call it (yell out, "I've got it!") so the other infielders know you are going for it. Get under the ball and catch it in your glove (Figure 6-3). Use your other hand over the glove to keep the ball from popping back out.

6-2: Always reach for the ball to field it out in front of you. Keep your head down and watch the ball go into your glove. Your throwing hand should cover the ball as it enters the mitt.

Infield Plays

Forced Out

A *forced out* is when a runner is forced to run, and an infielder, who has the ball, tags the bag before the runner gets there. Once you've made the forced out, you should be ready to throw the ball to another base in case of a double play.

Double Play

A *double play* is when the defense gets two outs on one hit ball. Here's examples of two double plays:

1. **There's a man on first. A ground ball is hit to the third baseman, who fields it and throws to second base.** The second baseman catches the ball and tags the bag for the first putout. The second baseman turns and throws to the first baseman who tags the bag before the batter gets there for the second putout.

2. **There's a man on first. A line drive is hit to first. The man on first breaks for second.** The first baseman catches the ball to put out the batter. Then touches the bag before the runner from first can get back to it, and the runner is put out, too.

6-3: Always make sure you can catch the pop fly before you call for it. Use both hands and try to catch the ball over your throwing shoulder.

6-4

6-4: It's the runner's job to try to break up a double play. That means he's going to try to knock you down with his slide. Get to the bag as quickly as possible, make the throw, and get out of the path of the runner. On a close play, you may have to take to the air.

6-5

6-5: Infielders have to get rid of the ball quickly to throw out fast baserunners. Don't drop your arm down. Bring it up and back to cut down on your release time. Occasionally, you may have to throw the ball sidearm.

Relay

When an outfielder throws the ball to an infielder who has moved into the outfield to make the catch, and that infielder throws the ball to another infielder to make the play, it's called a relay. This usually occurs when there's an extra-base hit to the outfield, and the throw to the base is too long for the outfielder to reach.

Cutoff Play

When an infielder intercepts (cuts off) a throw from an outfielder, it's called a *cutoff play*. You should cut off the outfielder's throw if you see that the throw is going to be too late to put out the runner.

Throwing in the Infield

When you field a ground ball, always try to put out the *lead runner* (one closest to home) (Figure 6-4). If there's no chance to put out the lead runner, throw to another base where there's still a chance for a putout. If there are no men on base, throw to first—it's the only play there is.

One of the hardest throws to make in the infield is when you only need to throw the ball a distance of six to eight feet to a baseman. If you throw the ball fast at this short distance, the baseman won't have time to move his glove to catch it. It's best to take a short step toward the baseman, draw your throwing arm back as far as your ear, aim at the baseman's chest, and flip the ball at the baseman by snapping your wrist forward as you release the ball.

Use the *sidearm throw* (throw with your arm out to the side of your body) when there's no time to make a regular throw (Figure 6-5). Don't use the sidearm throw unless you need it, because balls thrown sidearm can be hard to control.

Tagging the Runner

When you've got the ball on second or third, and a runner is sliding into base, you want to tag him without having him slide into you, and hurting you. Use the bag to protect you. Straddle it so your feet are out of the way of the runner, but you're still able to apply the tag.

6-6 and 6-7: Position yourself so that the tag will be straight down below you. Straddle the base to keep your legs out of danger of the runner. The tag should be very brief, and then get the glove out to show the umpire. You should always show the ump the ball whether you tagged the runner or not.

This also works well if you are receiving the ball from the opposite direction of the runner. For example, if you are receiving the ball at second base from the shortstop, simply open up your shoulders towards the ball, receive it, and apply the tag. As long as your feet are in the proper position to begin with, you don't have to worry about getting hit.

Tagging Out the Runner Drill

This drill teaches you how to catch the ball and make a good tagging motion. Practice it at first without a runner. Face the direction that the imaginary runner will be coming from and put one foot on each side of the bag. Have a teammate throw the ball to you. Catch the ball with the glove hand only and sweep the glove down to the dirt (Figure 6-6) in front of the base in a smooth, clockwise motion. The glove should only be on the ground for a split second. Bring your arm back up so the umpire can see the ball (Figure 6-7). After the tag, pivot away from the bag to avoid being held up by the runner. Keep practicing this drill until your tagging motion is very smooth. Then try the drill with a runner sliding into the base.

Practice, Practice, Practice

In order to develop good fielding skills, you have to practice a lot. One of the best ways to practice is to play baseball any time you get the chance, on the playground, with friends after school, or at the park. Do the drills in this chapter and play *One a Cat,* the game that's at the end of this chapter. Other ways to practice are to have a friend throw the ball for you to field. After you've fielded it, throw it right back to him just as you would if you were making a play in a game.

Make It Up, Play It Out

Here's a fun way to exercise all your baseball skills: running, fielding, throwing, catching, and hitting.

One a Cat

You need three or more players, a bat, a baseball, a glove for every player, a large open area, and one base. One player is the batter, one player is the pitcher, and the rest of the players are fielders. The pitcher pitches to the batter. If the batter hits the ball, he drops the bat and tries to make it to the base and back without getting put out. Outs are made just like in a regular game. When the batter makes an out, players rotate (the pitcher becomes the batter, the batter becomes a fielder, and a fielder becomes the pitcher). If the batter hits a fly ball and it's caught, then the player who catches it becomes the batter.

When there are more than four players, you can have two or more bases and two or more batters. The batter has to get to both bases and back home before he is put out. Because there is more than one batter, the first batter can stay on the first base and wait to move on until the next batter hits. The first runner is out if he doesn't make it home before all the other batters have batted.

Keep Focused

1. Balls hit to the infield include ground balls, pop flies, and line drives.
2. When a ball is hit on the ground, charge it, get in front of it, and use both hands to scoop it into your glove.
3. Get under a pop fly, call it, and catch it in your glove. Use your other hand to keep it from popping back out.
4. When you've fielded a ground ball and there are runners on the bases, you will usually want to throw to get the lead runner out. If there's no chance of getting the lead runner out, throw to another base.
5. On a relay play, the shortstop or second baseman is usually the relay man.
6. Always be aware of what's happening on the play and be ready to back up your teammates any way you can.

CHAPTER 7

The First Baseman

Find the bag, keep an eye on the action, get in position for the catch, and do it all while the tying run is barreling down the line! The first baseman's job isn't easy. He has to be able to move fast and think fast to cover the area around first base. The only players who see more action in a game are the pitcher and the catcher.

A great first baseman can scoop a throw out of the dirt as if his glove were a magnet. At the crack of the bat, he can move to the base and get set for the throw. He's on a bunt before the batter can drop his bat. To be a great first baseman you need: good hands, speed, brain power, and baseball sense. (Baseball sense is learned by playing the game. Reading this book will help, too.) All these qualities could be seen in the great first basemen of yesterday, like George Sisler and Lou Gehrig, and you can see these qualities in today's great players, like J.T. Snow and Andres Galarraga.

It's not absolutely necessary for a first baseman to be tall, but it helps if you are. A few extra inches means you can stretch farther to catch a wide throw.

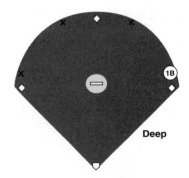

Deep

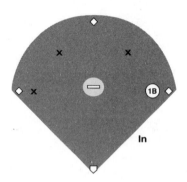

In

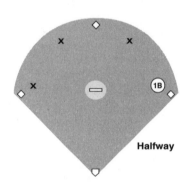

Halfway

Left, Right, Right, Left

A left-handed first baseman throws with his left hand and catches with his right. It's just the opposite for a right-handed first baseman. The left-handed first baseman has an advantage in fielding because his glove (on his right hand) is closer to the infield than the foul line, and most balls come to the infield. After he catches the ball, he doesn't need to turn his body in order to throw to second or third. He can also make a quicker tag on a runner who's trying to get back to first. The only time a right-handed first baseman has an advantage is when he's catching a ball that comes down the basepath.

First Baseman Fielding Positions

A first baseman uses four basic positions on the field. They are: deep, halfway, in, and holding a runner on.

Deep

When you are playing *deep*, position yourself near the edge of the outfield grass. This allows you to cover the foul line and maybe stop a hit coming down the baseline. The deep position is used most often in the late innings when your team has the lead and you want to protect that lead. It's also a good position to take if you face a strong batter who hits the ball hard.

In

When playing *in*, you want to be exactly on the infield grass line, ready to run toward the plate. This position is used to defend against a bunt or when the bases are loaded and you have to get the force at home plate. Make sure you're ready to field the ball and get rid of it quickly because the game is probably on the line.

Halfway

Playing *halfway* puts you halfway between deep and in. When you're halfway, you're set in position to make a force play at second base, throw home to get a runner trying to score on a ground ball, or field a bunt. Playing halfway cuts down your range a bit, but it also gives you other options instead of simply going to first base on a ground ball.

Holding a Runner On

With a *runner on* first, face the pitcher and put your right foot near the corner of the bag that faces the pitcher and your left foot on the foul line (Figure 7-1). Keep your knees bent, bend your elbows and hold your glove in front of you. If the pitcher throws to the plate, get off the bag and into the field to cover some territory. Make sure you get yourself into the ready position.

7-1: Keep the right foot on the base and stretch out with the left leg when holding a runner on. If the throw over is on the mark, allow the ball to come to you. Don't reach out to catch it.

Fielding the Ball

Ground Ball

When you get a grounder in the hole (space between you and the second baseman), and you can't get back to the bag, your pitcher should already be running toward first. Throw the ball a little ahead of him so he gets it a stride or two before he reaches the bag. This gives him time to watch the throw and still find the bag. If you have to throw the ball a long way, throw it overhand. If a shorter throw is needed, throw it underhand, stepping at your target, keeping your wrist stiff. Chase the ball after you throw it, so you'll be ready to grab it and make the play, in case the pitcher drops it.

Sacrifice Bunts

On the sacrifice bunt, get the lead runner out if possible. As soon as the pitch is released, charge forward. Your catcher should yell out the base you should throw to before you pick up the ball. The moment you pick it up, face the infield, in position to get rid of the ball fast. If you see that the lead man is going to be safe at the bag, don't risk a throw. Your pitcher or second baseman should be covering first. Get the sure out at first.

Pop Fly

Most fly balls that the first baseman catches are in front of him or off to his left in foul territory. If you see a pop-fly going back into shallow right field (the outfield territory beyond first base that is covered by the right fielder), let the right fielder have it if he calls you off. This is because the right fielder has a better angle to run for the ball than you do. Wave off the pitcher or catcher from pop flies that are easier for you to catch. On pop flies in foul territory, watch for fences and screens. Many first basemen run to the screen or fence first, then move away from it and catch the ball. This is a good way to judge whether the ball can be fielded.

7-2: If you don't have time to get back to the base when fielding a bunt, step and throw the ball over to the pitcher covering. Here, Mo Vaughn is close enough to toss the ball underhand. Make sure you step at your target, and lead the pitcher to the bag.

Underhand Toss Drill

Have a coach or teammate hit ground balls to your right side. Shuffle over, field the ball, step toward your target and toss the ball underhand to the pitcher. Always lead him with the throw because he's running over to cover first base (Figure 7-2). It should be a crisp toss to the chest of the pitcher.

Drags and Push Bunts

Drag bunts are when the left-handed batter bunts the ball down the first baseline and *push bunts* are when the right-handed hitter directs the ball toward first base. The ball usually rolls down the baseline and is hard to field. If it's hit past the pitcher, but doesn't have enough power to reach you in time to make the play, the best you can do is hurry to the ball and hope there's still a play to make.

Receiving the Throw

No matter where you are positioned, you should always be ready to catch the ball. When a ball is hit to the infield, get to the bag as fast as you can, while keeping track of the play. It's a big help if you can find the bag without having to look for it because you can keep your eyes and body facing the action on the field. Once you've played first base for a while, you will get a sense of where the bag is. As soon as you get to the bag, get in the ready position with both heels touching the bag. Let the throw decide how you catch the ball.

7-3: By stretching to the throw, you will receive the ball faster, and have a better chance of getting the runner out. See the throw first and where the ball is going before you stretch for it.

Stretch to Catch

When you're on first base, and the ball is coming to you, stretch your body to catch it (Figure 7-3). Put the foot opposite your glove hand on the bag. This will give you the longest reach. *Stretch* your glove hand up, keeping it in front of you. Don't go into the stretch position before the infielder has released the ball. If the throw comes in wild, you'll be off-balance and you won't be able to catch it.

Hard Catches

Many times, balls thrown to first are *hard to catch*. Infielders sometimes throw in a hurry or when they're off-balance. This is why you should play the ball, not the base. If the throw is wild, come off the bag and go for the ball.

Catching Bad Throws Drill

Stand about 30 feet away from a friend or teammate. Have him throw balls that land a little in front of you. Move your body in front of the ball, watching the ball all the way into your glove. Once you make the catch, pretend that you're throwing the ball on to another base and get ready to throw.

Think Fast

Knowing what to do on every kind of play will help you do the right thing, fast, in a game. Here's some situations that might come up and how you might want to react to them:

Runner on First?

Ask yourself, "Is he fast?" If he is, do everything you can to keep him close to the bag. If he's not real fast, you might want to move up the basepath with him as he takes his lead. But if the score is close, you might want to hold even a slower runner close to the base. If you have a big lead and it's late in the game, don't worry about the runner advancing. Play deep so you can field the ball to make a play on the batter.

Who's the Batter?

Watch the batter so you can learn about his abilities. Is he more likely to hit the ball to the right or to the left? If you know the answer to this question, play more toward that side. Is he fast? If he is, stay close to the bag. If he's not speedy, you can cover more territory.

What's the Pitch?

Know the pitches before they're thrown. If you can see the signals, that's great. If you can't, have your second baseman signal you when a breaking ball or some other off-speed pitch is coming. Because

Outside the Lines

SCOOP IT UP AND CHUCK IT
Slick fielding first baseman Keith Hernandez once said, "Being left-handed at first is a great advantage because I can scoop and then throw in one motion."

these pitches are easier to pull (go close to the foul line), move to the right.

   If an outside pitch is signaled, start moving left. For an inside pitch, start moving right. If the whole infield is thinking and moving like you, your team has an advantage over the batter.

7-4: Will Clark stretches a good distance to make this catch.

1. Being ready means watching the ball and taking the right stance. Bend your knees, get up on the balls of your feet, and hold your glove low.
2. When you're playing deep, position yourself at the edge of the outfield grass.
3. When you're playing in, stay on the infield grass line, ready to drive toward the plate.
4. When you're playing halfway, position yourself halfway between deep and in.
5. When you're holding a runner on base, put your right foot near the corner of the bag that faces the pitcher, and your left foot on the foul line. Face the pitcher.
6. Do your best to get all the plays to your right.
8. Play the ball, not the base.
9. Knowing what to do on every kind of play that can come up during a game will help you think fast.

CHAPTER 8

The Middle Infielders

The second baseman plays on the first-base side of second. The shortstop plays on the third-base side of second. Together, they defend the middle of the infield. They must be able to make hard catches, be able to move quickly in any direction, and be able to throw fast and accurately, even when throwing sidearm or off-balance. Their solid fielding abilities and their ability to work together are a very important part of a winning team.

Together, the second baseman and the shortstop are responsible for second base and all the territory between second and first, and between second and third. This means that they should field all the fly balls that come between either one of them and the pitcher's mound. They should also catch balls that fall close to second base. (Balls which go over their heads more than 10 feet should be fielded by the out-fielders.)

Deep

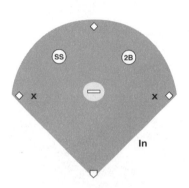

In

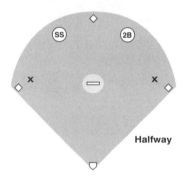

Halfway

Playing Deep

If there is nobody on the bases, the second baseman and shortstop play *deep*, meaning they position themselves at the back of the infield dirt. Playing deep makes them able to cover more territory.

Playing In

If there is a runner on third and the score is close, the second baseman and shortstop should play *in*, meaning they position themselves on the edge of the infield grass. This allows them to get the ball quicker, and gives them a shorter throw to the plate if the runner on third tries to go home.

Halfway

When his team is ahead, the coach might tell the second baseman and shortstop to play *halfway* (halfway between in and deep). Once the ball is hit, you have to make the decision where to make the throw. If the ball is hit hard to you, throw to home. (Because the ball gets to you fast, you might be in time to get it to the plate ahead of the runner.) If the ball isn't hit hard, you probably won't be able to get the out at third, but you might still be able to get the out at first, so throw to first.

Working Together

Before the game, the second basemen and the shortstop talk strategy and make decisions about which one will take certain responsibilities on certain plays. Here's some examples of how the second baseman and shortstop work together during a game:

Double Play

There's a runner on first and the ball is hit to the shortstop. The second baseman runs to the bag. The shortstop fields the ball and throws it to the second baseman who catches it for the forced out, then throws the ball to first base for the out there.

Double Play Drill

Stand on second base and have the shortstop feed you throws to get the force out. Have a runner slide into second as you relay the throw to first base. This will get you used to getting out of the way of the runner. Later, practice the same drill but have the second baseman feed the shortstop.

Defending the Steal at Second

In the higher levels of play, the second baseman and shortstop defend against the steal at second.

If it's a close game or tie score and there's a man on first, it's likely that he'll try to steal second to get into *scoring position* (second and third bases are considered scoring position because a runner can often get home from there). If the second baseman or shortstop thinks the runner on first is going to try to steal second, they signal to each other before the pitch to decide who will cover the bag. The one who's covering the bag moves closer to second, so he can get there in time to take the throw from the catcher. The one who's not taking the bag, backs up the bag (moves behind the base in case the one on the bag misses the throw). It's important to back up the bag because if the ball gets away, the runner might have time to go on to third.

8-1: When covering on the steal, position your feet so you have a clear path in front of the bag to tag the runner. The ball should be caught with your glove hand so you can quickly swipe a tag and show the umpire the ball. Here, Rickey Henderson looks like he has this throw beat.

Covering the Bag

If you're covering the bag, make sure you're close enough to the bag so you can get there in time for the throw. Break for the bag when you see the runner go. Get one foot on either side of the bag, bend your knees, and get both hands up and ready to receive the throw (Figure 8-1). When you make the tag, sweep your glove down so it meets the incoming runner as he slides in. Don't reach for him, let him slide into your glove and tag himself. As soon as you make the tag, get your glove back up and show the umpire your glove.

Force Play at Second

When there's a runner on first, and the ball is hit back to the pitcher, the pitcher will turn to throw to second to get the lead runner out. The second baseman and shortstop decide together before the play occurs who is going to cover second base when there's a forced-to-run situation.

The Relay Men

Although any infielder can move into the outfield to catch a ball from an outfielder and relay the ball to the infield, the second baseman and the shortstop are most often the relay men because of their position in the middle of the field. If the ball is hit to right field, the second baseman goes out for the relay. If the ball is hit to left field, the shortstop goes out for the relay. The second baseman and the shortstop decide before the game which one will go out for the relay if the ball is hit to center field.

The Second Baseman

Shorter Throw to First

The second baseman has a shorter throw to first base than the shortstop, so you have a little more time to get the throw off to first. On a ground ball, if there's no one on base, you should make sure the ball doesn't get by you. Even if you don't field the ball cleanly, you will still have time to throw the batter out at first base.

Double Play Danger

Because you play to the first-base side of second, when you run for the base, your back is toward first, and you're facing the shortstop. As soon as you receive the ball from him, you have to *pivot* (turn) to make the throw to first (Figure 8-2). While your back is turned toward first, the runner will be barreling down the basepath toward you. Even if the runner is already out because you've tagged the bag, he will still slide into you to try to make you miss your throw to first. Jump across or push back off the bag to avoid being hit, but always make sure you get that first out.

8-2: The double play pivot is more difficult for the second baseman because he has to change direction in his momentum. Once the ball is received at second base, plant and then push off with your right foot to get a strong throw over to first base.

Second Baseman Covering First

On a bunt, be ready to cover first base. The first baseman will be moving in to field the ball, so you go to first base to take the throw from him.

Ground Balls

When fielding ground balls, know the range of the first baseman. Try to get most of the ground balls to your left, which allows the first baseman to stay on the bag.

Pop Flies

Be ready to call the pitcher and the other fielders off a pop fly if you have the best angle on it (Figure 8-3). Go after all pop flies to shallow right and shallow center of the outfield until the outfielder calls you off. If you have to go after a ball into foul territory, always be aware of where the obstacles (fence, other players) are.

8-3: The second baseman has the responsibility of catching everything in the air he can get to behind first base. Call the first baseman if you're able to make the play.

The Shortstop

Longer Throw to First

Because the shortstop is farther from first than the second baseman, he has a longer throw to first. The average throw a shortstop makes to first base is 110 feet, but it can be up to 30 feet farther (Figure 8-4). You have to field the ball fast and get rid of it, fast. To do this, you need lightning-fast feet and good aim.

More Ground to Cover

The shortstop has the most ground to cover of all the infielders. You must be able to move to field balls up to 30 feet on either side of you. That's another reason why you need to be able to run fast.

Quick Throw Drill

This drill will train you to make the catch and get the throw off quickly. The second baseman and shortstop stand about 25 feet apart and throw the ball back and forth, fast, to each other's chest. When receiving the ball, reach out for it with both hands. Your feet should already be moving into position for the throw as you make the catch. It's important to reach for the ball with two hands. That way, by the time you bring your glove back to your body, your throwing arm already has the ball and is ready to fire.

8-4: Shortstops have a long throw to first when they're forced to use their backhand. Field the ball off your left foot, plant with the right foot, and push off for a strong throw to first base.

8-5: The double play turn for a shortstop is a much easier play because he's coming across the bag toward first base. When you come across after receiving the ball from the second baseman, make sure you stay away from the path of the runner.

Keep Focused

1. The second baseman plays on the first-base side of second.
2. The shortstop plays on the third-base side of second.
3. The second baseman and shortstop should catch fly balls that come between either one of them and the pitcher's mound.
4. If there's a runner on third, play in.
5. If there's nobody on base, play deep.
6. When playing halfway, make the decision where to throw after the ball has been hit.
7. When you're covering the bag, make sure you stay close enough to get there in time for the throw.
8. Decide before the game whether the second baseman or the shortstop will go out for the relay in center field.
9. If you're the second baseman, be prepared to cover first base on a bunt.
10. If you're the shortstop, you have to field the ball and throw to first, fast.

The Third Baseman

T he third baseman's job is to cover third base and the area around it. Third base is also known as the *hot corner* because so many hard-to-field balls are hit there and because the third baseman has a longer throw to first than the other infielders. A hit down the third-base line gets to the third baseman in no time at all. Even fielding a routine grounder is a real test of skills.

Third Baseman's Strategy

Know the Game Situation and the Batter

Knowing the game situation, and the batter can help you decide where to position yourself. For example, when a strong, right-handed hitter is up, play deep. If he's known to be a pull hitter, shade to your right to cover the foul line. When a left-hander is batting, shade toward second. If the game is tight and a steal of third is possible, stay close enough to the bag to get back quickly.

Know the Pitch

Know which pitch is coming. The change-up draws hits to the third-base side. On the other hand, the fastball is less often hit to third. If you know a fastball is coming, shade toward second base, to gain more ground.

Third Baseman Fielding Positions

There are three general positions for the third baseman: deep, in, and halfway.

Playing Deep

Playing *deep* means that you are positioned near the edge of the outfield grass. When you play deep, you have more time to catch a batted ball. Playing deep also means that most of your territory is in front of you and you can cover more ground (Figure 9-1).

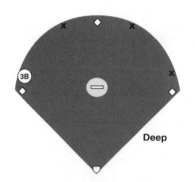

Deep

In

Playing *in* means that you are a few steps in on the infield grass. Play in when you think a bunt is coming. The less ground you have to cover, the faster you can field the bunt.

Halfway

Playing *halfway* means that you are playing even with the third base bag. It's the best place to play when the defense is looking to turn a double play (Figure 9-2).

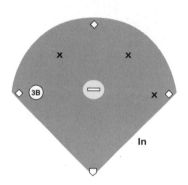

In

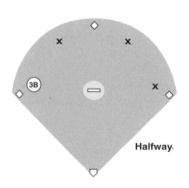

Halfway

Fielding the Ball

Get in the ready position before every play. Bend your knees, get up on the balls of your feet and get your glove down and open. Having your knees bent and being on the balls of your feet helps you get moving faster. Keeping your glove down is especially important at third base. Having your glove open and waiting allows you to grab a hit that might otherwise get by you.

Fielding Ground Balls

Try to field any ground ball you can reach. Never decide that another infielder will get the ball unless it's way out of your

In Figure 9-1, the third baseman is playing deep and toward the third baseline. You play deep either late in the game or with two outs to avoid giving up an extra base hit down the line. In Figure 9-2, he's playing even with the bag. He may play in this position to set up for the double play, or perhaps there's a batter with good speed at the plate.

range. Learn to field ground balls with your left foot slightly forward because then you only have to plant your weight on your right foot and throw, instead of taking an extra step.

Hot Corner Drill

Stand at third base, but facing the outfield. Have your coach hit regular ground balls to you. Just as he hits them, he should yell out "Turn!" Find the ball quickly and do your best to get your body in front of it. You may want to use tennis ball or soft baseballs for this drill.

Slow Rollers and Topped Balls

Slow rollers (ground balls that roll slow) and *topped balls* (balls hit on the top) often drop dead in the infield just beyond the reach of the pitcher but not close enough for the third baseman to easily field them. Since you will usually be playing closer in than the shortstop, you're responsible to go after these hard-to-field balls. Run toward the ball and field it off your left

You're regarded as a hitter who can do everything at the plate: hit for average, hit with power, hit to all parts of the field. What's the key to being a complete hitter?

The guys who considered the most complete hitters, the guys who are the most successful in hitting are the ones who can cover the whole plate. Whether the pitch is inside, outside, high, or low, they can put the bat on the ball and hit it hard somewhere.

How important do you think confidence is to a baseball player?

You have to have a lot of confidence in yourself whether it be in the field or at the plate. Even though baseball can be a very difficult game, you've got to believe you're going to succeed on every play. To be a winner, you've got to think like a winner.

Hitting is one of the most difficult acts in sports, but is it mentally challenging as well?

For me, hitting is almost all mental. I try to learn as much about the pitcher as possible. This way, I can think along with what he's thinking. If he got me out a certain way in the past, he'll probably try it again, so I can expect certain pitches to come.

What should a hitter be thinking when he goes up to the plate?

You've to think about being aggressive with the bat. Always look to swing the bat. If you're passive, the pitcher will take the action to you. You should take the action to the pitcher. You do this by taking your rips.

What advice do you have for a young ballplayer?

I would tell kids to practice and then practice some more. All big league players get to the major league level of play through hours of practice. We do so many drills that our bodies just react to what our brain tells us to do.

9-3: On a slow roller, field the ball coming in on the run. If you don't have time, you may have to throw on the run across your body. This is a very tough play, and should only be attempted when necessary.

foot. You may not have time to set your feet, and will have to throw on the run (Figure 9-3).

The third baseman should attempt to field all pop flies in his area. Wave off the pitcher and the catcher from balls you have a better angle on. Chase flies into the outfield until the outfielder calls you off, then stop and get out of the way.

Slow Rollers Drill

Take a position halfway. Have a teammate at the plate toss you some slow rollers. Move forward toward the ball. When you are a few feet from it, get down and grab it with both hands. As you come up, hop with both feet to turn yourself toward first, find your target, and throw the ball.

Plays at Third

Bunts

A bunt can happen at any time so always be on your toes. In a bunt situation, position yourself in to shorten the distance between you and the batter (Figure 9-4). If there's a man on first, charge the ball hard, field it with both hands, and throw. Listen to the catcher. He has the best view of the action and will tell you where to throw the ball.

With a runner on second, decide whether the pitcher should field the ball or not before the play. If he is fielding it, get to the base because he'll be throwing to you for a possible putout at third.

Squeeze Play

A *squeeze play* is when the batter bunts, hoping that the runner on third can get home. Look for a squeeze play when there are no outs or only one out, the team needs a run, and there's a fast man on third base. On the *suicide squeeze*, the runner sprints for home on the pitch. On the *safety squeeze*, the runner waits at third until he sees that the bunt is a good one before sprinting for home.

Defend against the squeeze play by holding the runner close to the bag. The closer you keep the runner to the bag, the better your team's chance of putting him out at the plate. When the pitch is delivered, run hard toward the plate. Field the ball and throw it to the catcher.

Stealing Third

When there's a very fast runner on second, look for him to try to steal third. When you see the runner break, get to the bag, get one foot on either side of it, and be ready to receive the ball from the catcher. After making the catch, put your glove (with the ball in it) between the incoming runner and the bag and let the runner tag himself. Get off the bag as soon as you make the tag and show the umpire the ball.

Cutoff Play

The third baseman almost never acts as a relay man, but he does have certain cutoff jobs on hits to left field. When there's a runner on second base and the batter hits a single to left field, move to a position in the infield grass on a line between home plate and the left fielder. If the left fielder throws home and there's no play, the catcher calls for the cutoff. Cut off the left fielder's throw and send the ball to another base or at least hold the batter on first. Move to the same cutoff position when a fly ball is hit to left field with a runner on third. The left fielder will throw home, expecting the runner on third to tag up to score after the catch. If the runner doesn't tag up, you can cut off the throw and hold the runner(s) on base.

9-4: On a bunt, the third baseman should already be playing in on the grass. Charge the ball, stop to field it, take a crow hop, and throw to first base. Planting your feet will enable you to throw the ball harder, and with better accuracy.

9-5: A third baseman has to possess very fast reflexes, and needs to be quick on his feet. Because he's so close to the hitter, he has to react almost instinctively. It's no secret why third base is nicknamed "the hot corner."

**MONEY IN THE BANK
AT THIRD BASE**
Don Money of the
Milwaukee Brewers set a
major league record with
261 consecutive errorless
chances at third base.
Money's streak started
September 28, 1973 and
lasted through July 16,
1974. When a ground ball
was hit to Money, a
putout was a safe bet.

Keep Focused

1. Third base is called the hot corner because so many hard-to-field balls are hit there and because the third baseman has the longest throw to first.
2. If you're right-handed, you have an advantage over a left-hander at third base.
3. Play deep when you think the batter is going to hit a fast, hard ball.
4. Play in when you think the batter is going to bunt.
5. Try to field any ground ball you can reach.
6. Run toward slow rollers and topped balls in a wide curve so when you come up for the throw, you'll be facing the first baseman.
7. Try to field all pop flies in your area.
8. Defend against the squeeze play by holding the runner close to the bag.
9. When there's a fast runner on second or when the other team is behind in the score and needs to advance the runner, look for him to try to steal third.

CHAPTER 10

The Outfield

T he *outfield* refers to the wide area around the diamond. The outfield also refers to the three outfield players: the right fielder, the left fielder, and the center fielder.

The outfield is a big place—it's three-quarters of the field. Because they have so much ground to cover, outfielders have to be very fast. You can become a good outfielder by learning and practicing the fielding basics that are included in this chapter. The harder you work to learn the basic skills, the more important you'll be to your team.

The Right Fielder

The right fielder's job is to cover the right side of the outfield, which is the area beyond first base from the right foul line to the area covered by the center fielder. If you're a right fielder, you have to throw the ball the farthest because most throws from the outfield will be to third base or home. If you're fast, your speed can help keep runners on base, because they know you can get the ball back to the infield quickly.

The Left Fielder

The left fielder's job is to cover the left side of the outfield, which is the area beyond third base from the right foul line to the area covered by the center fielder. Plays in left field happen very fast, so you need to be able to react fast.

The Center Fielder

The center fielder covers the area in the middle of the outfield beyond second base. He has more territory to cover than the other two outfielders. If you're the center fielder, you're the leader in the outfield and you're in on every play. Any ball you call for is yours, and if it's another outfielder's ball, you have to back him up.

Before the Game Begins

Before the game begins, check out the outfield. If you play right field or left field, take a couple of runs to the foul area on that side to get an idea of how large a territory you have to cover and how far it is to the fence. Check out the fence. What's it made of? Are there any strange angles that might give a ball a wild bounce? Are you able to climb it? Throw a few balls off the fence to see how they bounce. This will help you play the fence a lot smarter during the game.

Taking Your Position in the Outfield

Playing Shallow

Play *shallow* (close to the infield) when there's a runner on base and the score is close. An extra-base hit will win the game anyway, but you might be able to put out the runner on a shallow fly ball.

You should also play shallow if the batter is a small guy that drops a lot of singles into the shallow outfield and rarely hits a long ball.

Playing Deep

If the batter is a *slugger* (powerful hitter), it's a good guess that he'll hit the ball far, so play *deep* (closer to the fence). If you know the slugger is right-handed and that he's a pull-hitter (tends to hit to the left), shade towards left field. If the slugger is left-handed, and a pull-hitter, he'll hit toward right field so shade over in that direction.

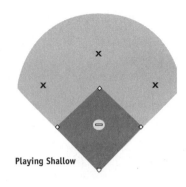

Playing Shallow

The Right Place at the Right Time

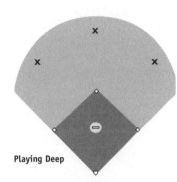

Playing Deep

You'll field the ball much faster if you can guess where the ball is going to come down and if you can get there before it comes. Here's how to make good guesses:

Judge the Ball

Judging the ball means guessing how fast and how far it will fly. To help you judge the ball, keep track of certain things:

Know the Wind Direction

A strong wind blowing in from the outfield will slow the ball down and cause it to fall sooner. A strong wind blowing toward the outfield will push the ball to travel farther. Check the wind direction every once in a while because it can change.

Play the Sun

Don't let the sun keep you from making a catch. When you are watching a ball and the sun is in your eyes, the bill of your baseball cap should help. If not, shade your eyes with your glove.

10-1: Every time a pitch is thrown, assume it's going to be hit to you. Be aware of what you need to do (where to back up, what base to throw to, where the cut-off man will be) before the play even happens.

Ready Position

Once you've decided on your position, take your stance in the ready position (Figure 10-1). As the ball approaches the plate, start moving forward.

Fielding the Ball

Fielding Fly Balls

After you've judged a fly ball, move to where you think it will drop. When there is time, angle your approach to the ball (Figure 10-2). Instead of running straight toward the infield on a short fly, and then turning your body after the catch to make the throw to the base, angle your approach, so that you come out of the catch already facing the base you want to throw to. Don't forget to call the other fielders off.

Deep Fly Balls

When you chase a fly ball all the way to the fence, but can't quite make the catch, get ready to catch it as it rebounds off the fence. It's hard to tell which way the ball will bounce, so stay back and be ready to react to it.

Sinking Line Drives

A *sinking line drive* is one that drops lower as it flies. Turn your palm up and catch the ball out in front of you. Always keep your body in front of the ball.

Fielding Ground Balls

How you field ground balls depends on the game situation. If no runners are advancing, charge the ball and get down on one knee to be sure it doesn't get by you (Figure 10-3). If a runner is advancing on the grounder, get the ball as fast as you can. Charge the ball, get your glove down low, and field the ball with both hands (Figure 10-4).

To get off a quicker throw, try to field the ball with your left foot forward if you're right-handed, or with your right foot forward if you're left-handed. That way, you can go right into your throw without having to take a step first for balance.

Charge all ground balls, even ones hit to an infielder, just in case the infielder fails to stop the ball.

Ground Ball Fielding Drill

Stand anywhere in your area of the outfield. Have one teammate cover first base and have another teammate stand about 30 feet away from you, toward the infield. Have him toss you some ground balls. Watch how the ball is moving, charge it, get down on one knee, catch it with both hands, and throw it to first as fast as you can. After you've practiced fielding several ground balls, shift your positions on the field (you move in to cover first, the first baseman moves out to throw, and the thrower moves back to field). Keep up

10-2: Position yourself to catch the ball over your throwing shoulder with two hands. If you have time, stand a few steps back from where the ball will land so you have to move forward to catch it and gain momentum for your throw.

10-3

10-4

10-5

10-3 through 10-5: There are three ways to field a ground ball in the outfield. The first way (10-3) is to go down on one knee. Use this when you have time and want to make sure the ball doesn't get past you. The second option (10-4) is to field the ball like an infielder. This is when you want to get the ball back to the infield quickly so the runners don't advance. The third method (10-5) is "Do or Die" which means you field the ball on the run. This is used when you're trying to throw a runner out who is going/trying to take an extra base. It's risky to use this method because you're fielding the ball with one hand off your glove-side leg. If the ball takes a bad hop, your body isn't there to block the ball. The "Do or Die" should only be used in critical situations.

the drill until everyone has had a chance to practice as the fielder. Repeat the drill, throwing to different bases.

Making the Throw

Remember that your first job is to catch the ball, and your second job is to throw it. If you throw the ball before you have a good hold on it, you might make an error.

The best way for the outfielder to throw the ball is with a strong, overhand motion. Keep your non-throwing shoulder and your head facing your target. Take a short hop when you release the ball. Throw the ball hard and low. A low ball is easier for the infielders to handle and harder for the runners to judge. Make sure to follow through by letting your arm continue its motion after you release the ball.

10-6: It's important to get the ball back to the infield quickly. If you take too long, the runners can take an extra base on you.

Getting the Throw Off Fast

If there's a runner on base, it's important to get the throw off quickly (Figure 10-6). Watch the ball. Take a step or two back from where the ball will drop. Then move forward to make the catch. This gives you forward momentum (motion) for your throw. Catch the ball with your body already turned in the direction you want to throw.

Outfielder Footwork Drill

Stand about 15 feet away from another player who has the ball. Face the other player and stand in the ready position. Your partner yells, "Ball!" and points over your left or right shoulder. If he points to your right shoulder, turn your hips to the right, take a step back with your right foot, turn and run, while looking back over your left shoulder for the ball (Figures 10-7 and 10-8). Run to the spot where the ball is coming down and catch it over your throwing shoulder. Practice making the turn-and-run to the left and to the right. Then throw for your partner so he can practice, too.

Working as a Team in the Outfield

The best outfielders play together as a team. They talk to each other all the time. The center fielder is the leader, but each outfielder knows his own job and what to expect from the others.

Backing up the Bases

When the batter bunts, the outfielders race in to back up the bases. The right fielder backs up first, the center fielder backs up second, and the left fielder backs up third.

If there are men are on the bases and you are not needed to field a ball in the outfield, run in to cover a base.

Backing up the Infielders

On any ball hit to the infield, the outfielders should come in to back up the play. Stopping a missed grounder from dribbling into the outfield can prevent a runner from taking an extra base.

On the double play, an outfielder should back up second base whenever possible.

Backing Up Your Fellow Outfielders

Whenever you can, get in position to back up another outfielder. If he knows you're there to stop the ball if he misses it, he can go all out for the catch.

Staying Alert in the Outfield

Staying on top of the game can be hard in the outfield. Sometimes a few innings go by without you ever touching the ball. And because you're so far away from the infield activity, you can feel all alone out there.

To stay alert, make a special effort to keep your mind on what's happening in the infield. Think along with the pitcher, watch what kinds of pitches he's throwing, and think how you might be needed on the play.

10-7 and 10-8: The most important step on a fly ball to the outfielder is his first step. Start in the ready position (10-7). When a ball is hit in the air in your direction, you should take a drop step (10-8). Open up to the side on which the ball is hit, and run to the spot where it will come down.

Make It Up, Play It Out

Here's a game that lets you practice your outfield moves. You also get some batting practice at the same time.

Call It First

You need five or more players, a bat, a baseball and glove for each player, and a field. One player bats, one player pitches, and the rest of the players spread out in the outfield. Before the pitch, the batter calls out who he is going to hit to. If he hits to that person, either on the ground or in the air, he continues to bat. If he misses, the players shift positions (the batter goes to right field, the right fielder goes to center, the center goes to left field, the left fielder becomes the pitcher, and the pitcher goes to bat). Keep playing until everyone has had a chance to field several balls.

Keep Focused

1. If you're the right fielder, cover the area beyond first from the right foul line to the area covered by the center fielder.
2. If you're the left fielder, cover the area beyond third base from the right foul line to the area covered by the center fielder.
3. If you're the center fielder, you're the leader in the outfield. Cover the area in the middle of the outfield beyond second base.
4. Check out the outfield before the game begins.
5. Play shallow when there's a runner on base and the score is close.
6. Play deep when the batter is a real slugger.
7. Know the pitch so you can guess where the ball might be hit.
8. Know the wind direction, and which hits are hardest to judge.
9. Keep the sun out of your eyes.
10. To field a sinking line drive, let it bounce once. Catch it by letting it bounce up into your glove.
11. Make sure you have a good hold on the ball before throwing it.
12. Get the throw off to the infield as fast as you can.

Glossary

Bag—A stuffed canvas base used at first, second, and third.

Balk rule—When there are one or more runners on base, the pitcher is not allowed to stop the pitch once he has started his windup. A pitcher can balk by stopping his throw, dropping the ball, or throwing the ball to a base. If the pitcher balks, each runner advances one base.

Ball—**1.** Any ball pitched outside the strike zone that the batter doesn't swing at. It's also a ball if the batter doesn't swing and the pitch hits home plate or the ground before entering the strike zone, or if the batter is hit by a ball thrown outside the strike zone. **2.** A baseball.

Barrel—The fattest part of the bat, near the top.

Base—There are four bases, one at each corner of the infield. The bases are called, first, second, third, and home plate. First, second, and third bases (also called bags), are stuffed, rectangular pads, fastened to the ground. Home plate is a white, five-sided, rubber plate set level in the ground between the batter's boxes.

Base on balls—When, after four balls, the batter walks to first base.

Bat—A tapered stick-like object that is used to hit the ball. Bats can be either wood or aluminum. Bats for young players are from twenty-six inches to thirty-one inches long and weigh less than two pounds.

Batter—An offensive player who stands in the batter's box to swing at the ball.

Battery—The name given to the pitcher and catcher together.

Batter's boxes—Two four-foot by six-foot rectangles, one on each side of home plate, where the batter stands to swing at the ball. Right-handed batters use the box to the left of the plate. Left-handed batters use the box to the right of the plate.

Batting order—The order in which a team's players come to bat. The batting order must be written down and given to the umpire before the game. Also called the lineup.

Breaking pitch—A pitch that breaks (moves) to one side or the other as it approaches the batter.

Bunt—A ball that is pushed with the bat so it travels only a few feet into the infield. A bunt for the purpose of getting the batter on first is called a *base hit bunt*. A bunt for the purpose of advancing a runner, even thought he batter, himself, is out is called a *sacrifice bunt*.

Catcher—The defensive player who crouches behind home plate and receives the ball from the pitcher when it is not hit by the batter.

Catcher's box—The area behind home plate where the catcher is positioned.

Center fielder—The defensive player who covers the middle of the outfield beyond second base.

Chair stance—A stance used by the catcher when there's a pitch coming. The pitcher is crouched with his weight forward on the balls of his feet as if he is about to sit down in a chair.

Change-up—A pitch that's thrown as a change from the fast ball. The change-up looks at first like a fastball, but travels much slower.

Coach—A manager's assistant. There can be more than one coach for a team. Coaches teach hitting, pitching, and fielding.

Coaching boxes—Two rectangular areas, one near first base, and the other near third base, where coaches stand to direct their team's runners.

Curveball—A pitched ball that curves before reaching the batter.

Cutoff play—When there are runners on the bases and a ball hit to the outfield is thrown by an outfielder toward a base, but an infielder intercepts (cuts off) the throw and throws the ball to a different base.

Defense—When your team is playing defense, you are playing in the field and the other team is at bat.

Deep—That part of an infielder's or outfielder's territory that's farthest from home plate.

Delivery—The style in which a pitcher throws, or delivers the ball. On the *full, overhand delivery*, the pitcher releases the ball when his arm is straight up in the air. On the *three-quarters, overhand delivery*, the pitcher releases the ball when his arm is above his shoulder and just in front of his head On the *sidearm delivery*, the pitcher releases the ball when his arm is to the side of his body at the height of his ribs. On the *submarine delivery*, the pitcher throws the ball underhanded and low.

Double—A hit that allows the batter to reach second base.

Double play—A defensive play in which two runners are put out on one hit ball.

Dugout—A shed, sunk into the ground, where players sit when they are not on the field. There are two dugouts, one near first base and one near third base. Professional ballparks and some other fields have dugouts. Youth baseball fields don't always have dugouts.

Error—When a member of the defensive team makes a fielding or throwing mistake that allows a runner to advance a base or to score.

Extra-base hit—A hit that's good for more than one base.

Fair ball—A ball that is hit into fair territory. On fair balls, the batter and any other players who are already on base can advance.

Fair territory—The area inside the foul lines.

Fastball—A ball that is pitched fast and hard. Also called a hummer. On a *rising fastball*, the ball seems to rise in the air as it approaches the batter. On a *sinking fastball*, the ball sinks in the air as it approaches the batter.

Field—The playing field for a baseball game is made up of an infield, an outfield, and foul territories.

First baseman—The defensive player who covers first base and the area around it.

Fly ball—A batted ball that travels high in the air.

Forced out—When a runner is forced to run and he's put out by the infielder tagging the bag before he (the runner) gets there.

Forced to run—When there's a runner on first, or runners on first and second, or runners on first, second, and third, and a fair ball hits the ground, each runner must advance to the next base because two runners can't be on the same base at the same time.

Foul ball—A ball that's hit into foul territory. A foul ball is a strike, except when a batter already has two strikes. A batter can't strike out on a foul ball.

Foul lines—The two lines that start at home base and run past first and third bases to the far edges of the outfield.

Foul territory—Any area outside the foul lines.

Game situation—The score, number of outs, inning, count, and number of men on the bases.

Glove—A special glove used for catching baseballs. Gloves are made of leather pieces that are stitched together along the outer edges to form a pocket over the palm. Gloves have separations for the fingers.

Grand slam—When you hit a home run with the bases full, scoring four runs.

Ground ball—A hit ball that bounces or rolls along the ground. Also called a grounder.

Halfway—The middle part of an infielder's or outfielder's territory.

Hit—A batted, fair ball that allows the runner to reach a base safely.

Home plate—A white, five-sided, rubber plate set level with the ground between the batter's boxes. Home plate is the last in a series of four bases that must be touched, one after another, to score a run.

Home run—A hit that allows the batter to round all the bases for a score.

Home team—The team on whose field the game is played. The home team bats last each inning

In—That part of an infielder's or outfielder's territory that's nearest home plate.

Infield—A square area of the field with a base in each corner. Also called the diamond.

Infield fly rule—When there's less than two outs and one or more runners are forced to run, and the batter hits a pop fly hit in the infield, he's out, whether the ball is caught or not.

Inning—An inning is the length of time necessary for each team to have a turn at bat. There are nine innings in a professional baseball game. A youth baseball game has less than nine innings.

Inside pitch—A pitched ball that passes inside the plate, close to the batter's body.

Knuckleball—A ball pitched with the knuckles on the ball. A knuckleball does not have spin so it tends to flutter in the air, making it hard for the batter to hit.

Lead runner—When there is more than one runner, the one closest to home is the lead runner.

Left fielder—The defensive player who covers the outfield area beyond third base from the left foul line to the area covered by the center fielder.

Line drive—A batted ball that flies straight and low at least as far as the infield before bouncing or being caught.

Major leagues—The professional teams that belong to the American League and the National League.

Manager—The manager makes decisions on the batting order and the game plan and is in charge of the team during a game.

Minor leagues—The leagues made up of teams that are used for training promising professional players who might later advance to major league teams. Some minor league teams are associated with certain major league teams. These minor league teams are called farm teams.

Mitt—A special mitt used for catching baseballs. Mitts are made of leather pieces stitched together along the outer edges to form a pocket over the palm. Unlike gloves, mitts do not have separations for the fingers.

Offense—When your team is playing offense, they are at bat.

On-Deck circle—A circle where the batter warms up when he is next in line to bat. In professional ballparks there are two on-deck circles, one between each of the dugouts and home plate.

Out—When a batter makes three strikes, or when the team in the field catches a fair or foul ball before it touches the ground, or when a fielder tags a runner with the ball before he reaches base safely or tags the base in front of the runner when he's forced to advance.

Outfield—The wide area surrounding the diamond from first to second base and from second to third base. In professional ballparks, there's a fence at the edge of the outfield. The shape and size of the outfield can vary from field to field.

Outside pitch—When a pitched ball passes outside the plate (the side opposite the batter's body).

Pick off—When a catcher makes a sudden throw to a base and catches the runner off the base for a putout.

Pitch—A throw by the pitcher, either through or near the strike zone, with a batter at the plate.

Pitcher—The player who stands on the pitcher's mound and pitches (throws) the ball through the strike zone to the catcher who is behind home plate.

Pitcher's mound—The raised area in the infield where the pitcher stands. The mound is 10 inches high at its highest point.

Pitcher's rubber—A rubber rectangle, six inches by twenty-four inches that sits on the pitcher's mound. The pitcher has contact with the rubber when he makes a pitch.

Pitchout—A pitch thrown wide of the plate so the batter can't reach it and so the catcher has a clear throw to a base to pick off a runner trying to steal. The wide pitch is called as a ball.

Pop fly—A hit ball that pops up high in the air in the infield, above, to the left, or to the right of the batter's box.

Professional baseball player—A player who earns his living by playing baseball.

Punch and Judy hitter—A batter who hits a well-placed ball but without much power.

Putout—A defensive play that sends the runner or batter back to the bench.

RBI—Run batted in. A batter earns an RBI when a run is scored because he makes a hit, gets a walk, or gets put out (except when he hits into a double play).

Ready position—A stance taken by fielders with knees bent, weight on the balls of the feet, and the glove held low in front of the body.

Relay—When an outfielder, deep in the outfield throws the ball to an infielder, who comes into the outfield to catch it, then relays (throws) it to another infielder who makes the play.

Right fielder—The defensive player who covers the outfield area beyond first base from the right foul line to the area covered by the center fielder.

Run—A score. When a runner touches home plate after advancing from first, to second, to third, touching each base in turn.

Rundown—When a runner is caught between bases with a defensive player on each side of him.

Sacrifice—When the batter hits the ball in order to get one of his teammates to the next base, even though the batter, himself, gets put out.

Safe—A runner is "safe" when he reaches a base without being put out.

Score—A run.

Screwball—A pitch that curves in the opposite direction of the curveball. Also called a reverse curveball.

Second baseman—The defensive player who covers second base and the area from second base toward first base.

Set position—One of two legal positions used by a pitcher.

Shortstop—The defensive player who covers the area between second and third base.

Single—A hit that allows the runner to advance one base.

Slide—When a runner, sprinting toward base, drops to the dirt and slides the last few feet to the bag. A *hook slide* is when the runner slides with his body away from the base and hooks the bag with his foot. A *straight-in slide* is when the runner slides with one leg doubled underneath him with the other leg outstretched to touch the bag.

Slider—A pitch that looks like a fastball until it gets three or four feet in front to the batter, then breaks slightly, making it hard for the batter to hit with the barrel of the bat.

Slow roller—A ground ball that rolls slowly.

Spin—A ball with spin turns while it flies through the air.

Squeeze play—A play where the batter hits a bunt in hopes that the runner on third can get home. A *suicide squeeze* is when the runner breaks for home on the pitch. A *safety squeeze* is when the runner waits to break from home until he sees that the bunt is good.

Steal—When a runner takes a lead and sprints for the next base as the pitcher goes into his windup. On a *delayed steal,* the runner waits until the catcher throws the ball to the pitcher before trying to steal. A *double steal* is when two runners steal bases on the same play.

Strategy—1. The game plan. 2. Making decisions during play based on knowing the game situation, field conditions, and strengths and weaknesses of the opponents.

Strike—When a batter swings at a pitch and misses, or doesn't swing at a pitch that comes through the strike zone.

Strike zone—The area above home plate that is between the batter's armpits and knee tops.

Strikeout—When a batter must go back to the bench after getting three strikes.

Sweet spot—An area on the barrel of the bat a few inches from the top that gives the best hit on the ball.

Switch-hitter—A player who bats right-handed or left-handed, depending on whether the pitcher is a righty or a lefty.

Tag—1. When a fielder uses the ball, or his glove with the ball in it, to touch a runner who is off the base. 2. When a fielder who has the ball, touches the bag before the runner gets there on a force play.

Tag up—When a runner tries to advance to the next base after a fly ball is caught.

Taking a lead—When a runner moves off base toward the next base before the ball is pitched.

Texas leaguer—A looping fly ball that drops just beyond the infield.

Third baseman—The defensive player who covers third base and the area around it.

Topped ball—A ball that's hit on it's top. A topped ball is driven to the ground.

Triple—A hit that allows a runner to advance three bases.

Umpire—An official who enforces the rules of the game and who calls balls and strikes. In a professional baseball game there are four umpires, one at home plate, and one near each base.

Windup—1. One of two legal pitching positions. 2. The movement of the pitcher's arms as he goes into his pitch.

World Series—A series of games between the American League championship team and the National League championship team to determine the world champion. The first team to win four games, wins the series.

Index